Olive Oil

FOREWORD by the President of IPEPO

Spanish olive oil has been produced and treasured for centuries. First used to light Ancient Egyptian temples, it has become one of the world's most valuable cooking products. Spain is proud of its international role as a major olive oil producer. For over twenty years IPEPO has promoted the use of Spanish olive oil for cooking. It is not therefore surprising that the Institute is the sponsor of this book about the liquid gold of Spain, featuring an expert selection of recipes involving Spanish olive oil, some regarded as classical dishes in many parts of the world. But this book is much more than a collection of recipes. Apart from background reflections on the illustrious olive and its versatile oil, every recipe in the two main sections of the book carries a nutritional analysis. This unusual feature will be of help and interest to those who are on calorie controlled diets or those who simply like to know the value of what they are eating. I believe this book will prove a useful guide to healthy, interesting and even adventurous cooking whatever the level of culinary skill and experience.

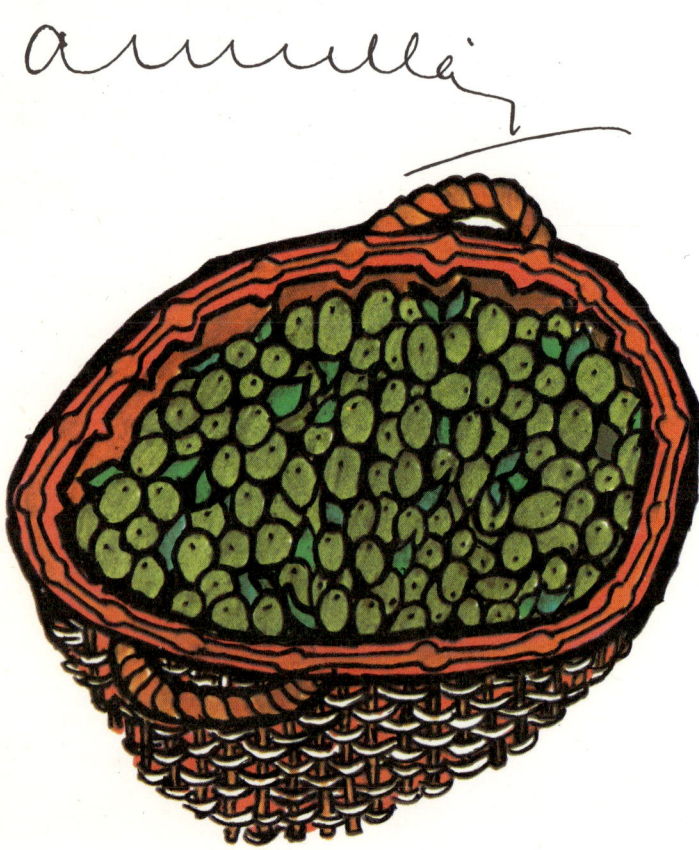

Dietary note
As there are variables which cannot be precisely calculated—the weight of three medium-sized vegetables for instance—the nutritional analyses are based on average size and weight. Where lower and upper limits are given (eg 4 to 6 helpings, 2/3 large onions) the calculations have been based on the larger amount. Other variations are covered by an additional note to the recipe.

Editorial consultant G C B Andrew FAIE, MIPR, MBIMA
Design consultant   Raymond E Meylan MSIA
The producers acknowledge valuable assistance from Elizabeth Macgregor

Published by Instituto para la Promocion
Espanola de los Productos del Olivar (IPEPO) Madrid
Presidente: Alfredo Jimenez-Millas
Director: Dr. Luis Patac de las Traviesas

Designed by Artes Graphicae Limited, London
Produced in England by Leonard A Kingsman
in association with Artes Graphicae Limited
for the Institute for the Promotion of Spanish
Olive Oil Products, Madrid

Printed by James Cond Limited,
London and Birmingham

© IPEPO Madrid and London

Contents

From Ancients to Astronauts	7
The Alchemy of Liquid Gold	11
Nutrition, Diet and Health Dr R Gordon Booth	16
Around the World in 40 Dishes Madame Simone Prunier	26
Home Cooking with Olive Oil Marguerite Patten	66
Top Chef's Choice	108
Housewife's Choice	118
Index to Recipes	124

6

Gilmore C B Andrew

From Ancients to Astronauts

As there is no evidence that the Garden of Eden contained an olive tree, the olive is probably the second oldest extant cultivated fruit. Fable and fantasy apart, there is no doubt at all that this venerable tree has shared Man's world for something like 5000 years. The genus is old and revered with a distinguished history and significance in mythology, theology, legend, medicine, cosmetics and gastronomy that no other fruit, certainly not the puny apple, can match. It is fact not conjecture that the olive was cultivated in Crete and Asia Minor in 3500 BC. We know that temples 5000 years ago were lit by lamps fuelled by olive oil. The Ancient Egyptians developed a method of extracting the oil that is basically the same today. And in our own Space Age the nutritious golden liquid has played the distinctly modern role of convenience food on board the first spacecraft to the Moon.

The precise origins of the olive tree are shrouded in doubt: Persia, the Valleys of the Nile and Jordan, Mesopotamia each have their advocates. The best we can say with certainty is that cultivation began a long, long time ago in the near East and spread slowly westward to Spain along the shores of the Mediterranean, the region that produces almost the entire world output of olive oil. It was propagation village by village, a slow-burning fuse of knowledge spreading across the centuries and countries. Many races, people of differing religious, ethnic and cultural backgrounds took part in this propagation. Phoenicians, Greeks, Jews, Carthaginians, Romans, Arabs, Spaniards— to all the olive became a tree of life and olive oil as basic a human need as daily bread.

Olive oil does more than span civilisation from Ancient Egypt to the Space Age: it cuts across the social spectrum, too, for the rich man in his luxury penthouse or five star hotel and the peasant in his humble Mediterranean hut will share the culinary largesse of the liquid gold.

About the olive's origins there may be doubt; about its longevity none at all. The tree is remarkably resistant to disease and tough enough to withstand prolonged drought conditions. It is not phenomenal but quite common to find an extant, very much alive tree that has survived a thousand years.

Nor is it really surprising that such a venerable tree should play a prominent role in mythology and history, legend and religion and should have become a universal symbol shared by peoples of contrasting races and creeds.

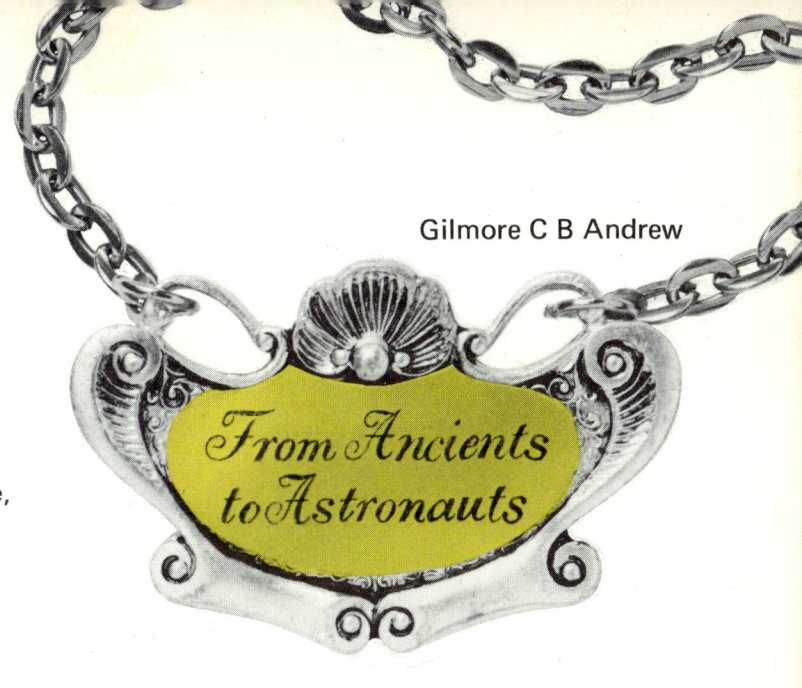

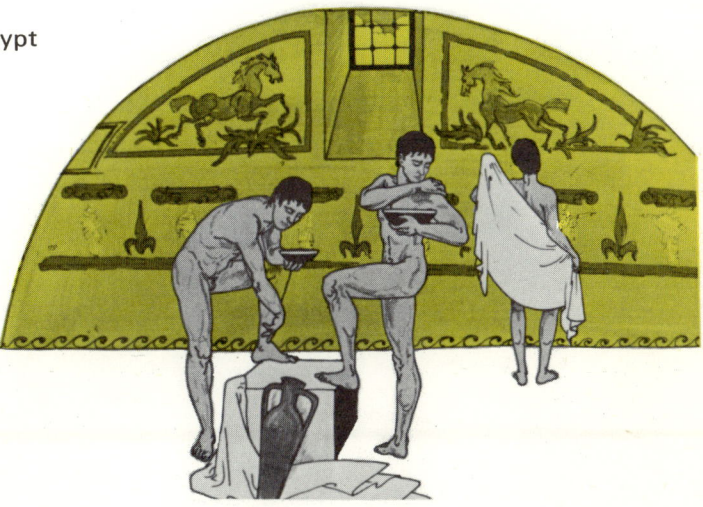

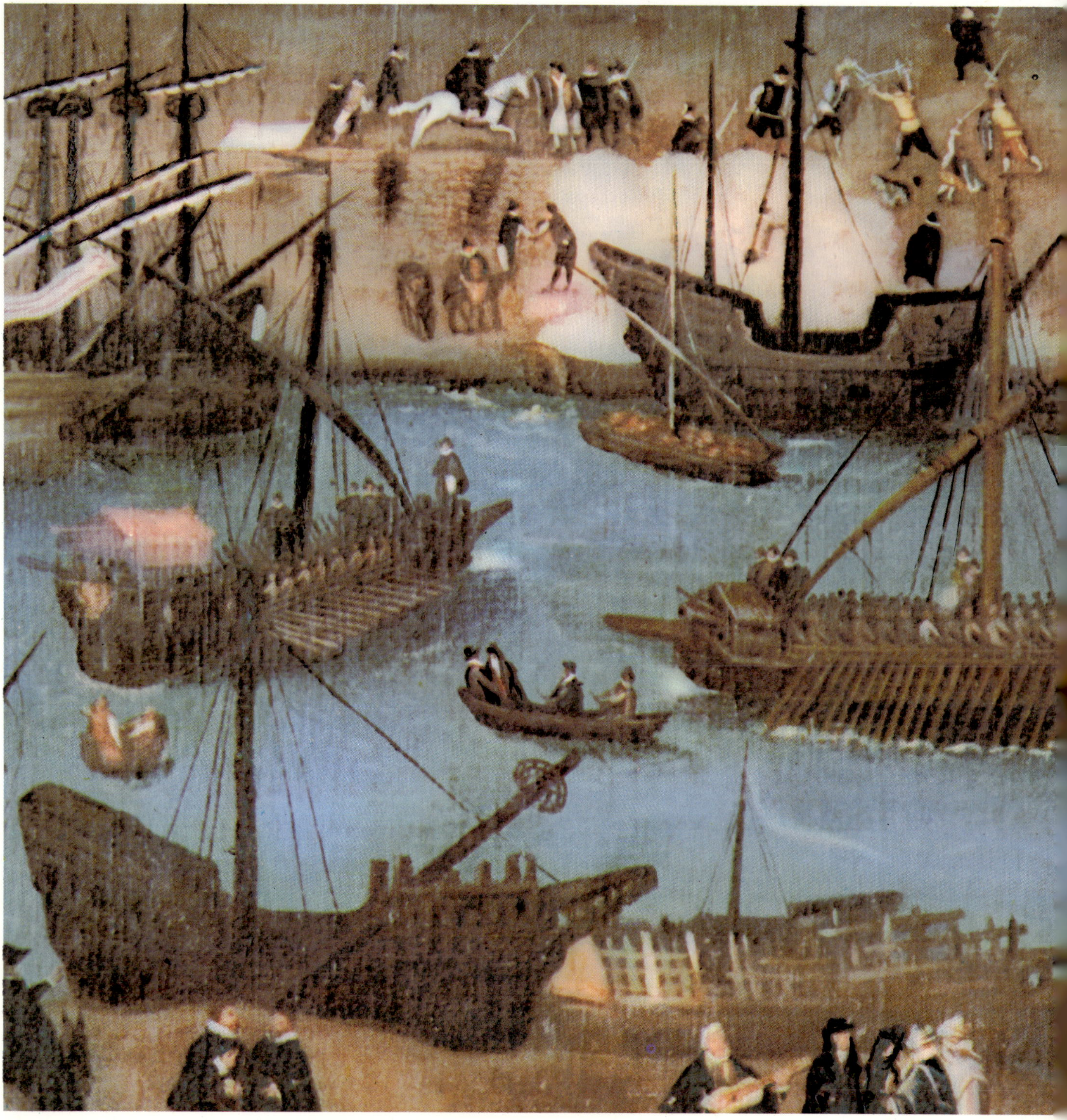

Children the world over know the significance of the Mount of Olives, that it was an olive branch the dove brought back to the Ark, proving to Noah that the waters were subsiding and survival was at hand.
Ever since in any language the olive branch has been the symbol of peace and goodwill. It comforted Noah and in our time inspired a famous work of art by Picasso.
The American War of Independence produced the Olive Branch Petition, an official plea from Congress to George III on behalf of the colonists. The Petition, though personally brought to London by Richard Penn, descendant of the legendary William, proved abortive for the King refused to accept it under any circumstances.
In another time and plane, Athena, Goddess of Wisdom, chose the olive as her gift to mankind and in return for this generosity the benefactors named a great classical city after her. The winners of Olympic and Pan-Hellenic Games as well as victors in Roman arenas were crowned with wreaths of olive branches.
In the Book of Judges (chapter 9 verse 7) the story is told that the trees wished to honour the olive, so distinguished a member of their species, by electing it the King of Trees. The olive declined because the mission God had entrusted to it was too important to be distracted by the chores of government, by the mundane responsibility of dominium over mere trees.
A touch of vanity, indeed, but indicative of the olive tree's significance in the eyes of that experienced crowner of kings, the human race. Little wonder, then, that Athena's choice of supreme gift for Man was not gold, precious stones or other material riches, but the fruit from which "an extraordinary liquid could flow to serve as food for Man, to alleviate his wounds, strengthen his body and lighten his night". Athena in her abundant wisdom was indeed bequeathing gold but of a different, vegetable not mineral kind.
Olive oil has been an indigenous produce of Spain for several thousand years. At the zenith of the Roman Empire, Spanish ships transported olive oil to Rome. Clay vessels of proven Spanish origin, stamped with the seals of the exporters, have been unearthed in Italy.
The olive was a major crop for the Romans in 600 BC and its oil an essential part of Greek bathing ritual in Homer's time some three hundred years earlier.
In worlds ancient and modern, olive oil has indeed proved the most versatile of juices.

10

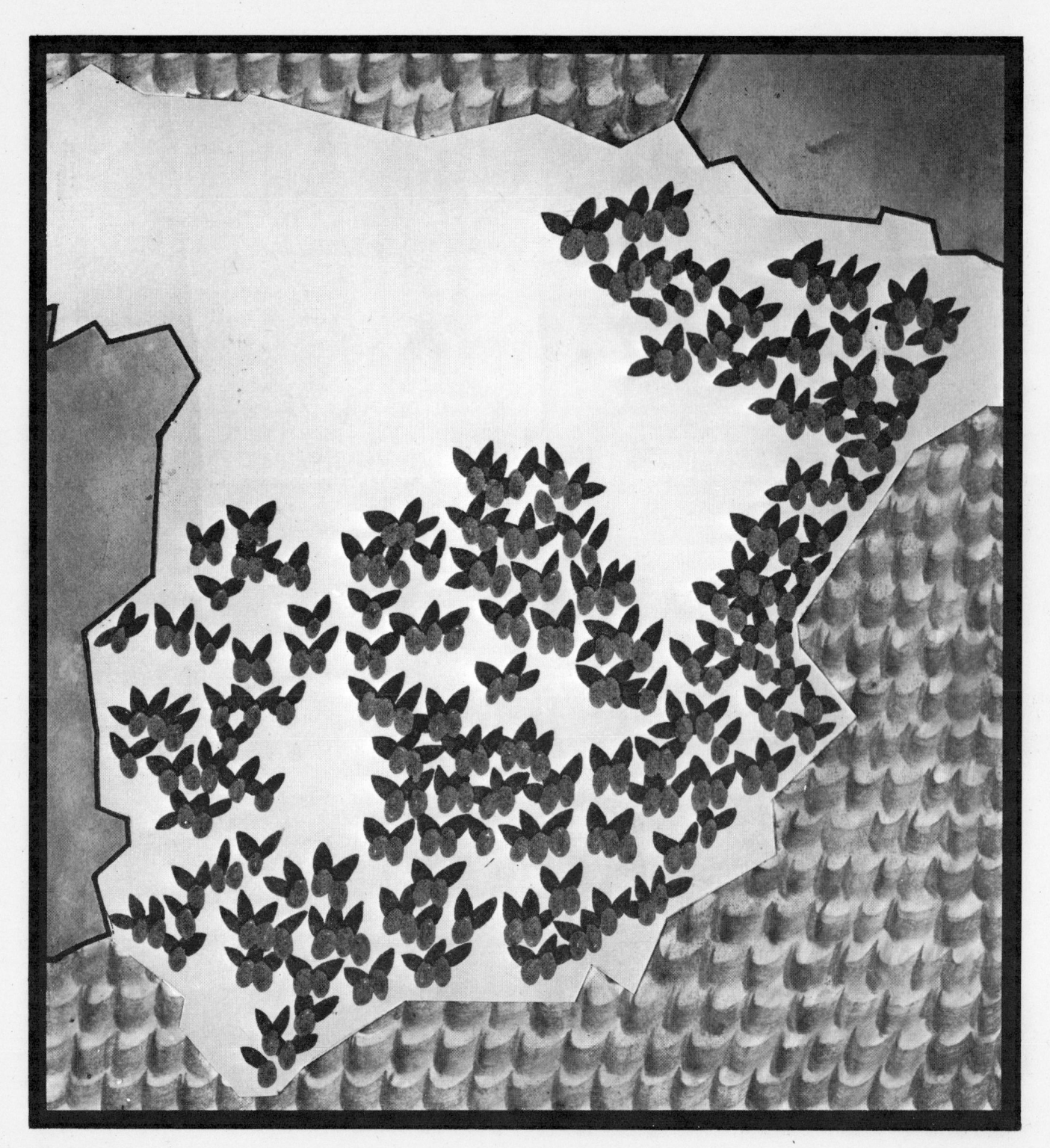

The Alchemy of Liquid Gold

All but three per cent of the world's olive trees, some eight hundred million trees, are concentrated in the Mediterranean area. Of these one quarter or 200 million trees are to be found in Spain. Spain, in fact, was also responsible for the introduction of the olive tree to the New World, for 16th century Spanish missionaries took the tree to Peru, Chile, Argentina, Mexico and later California. Today Spain turns 95% of her olive production into oil and is the world's largest exporter. The country's handsome counterpane of olive groves covers more than two million hectares, strategically situated in the regions most suited to the olive's wellbeing, in geographical terms somewhere between 30° and 45° N. The olive is a fussy species in some ways as perhaps any tree with its pedigree and past is entitled to be. It rarely gives fruit before it is ten years old and does not reach maturity for another fifteen. It will provide its best crop in a rainfall of over 500 millimetres falling between October and May. The marvellous alchemy of sun, rain and soil that contribute to the production of that other liquid wonder of the Spanish world, sherry, is also the open secret behind Spain's 200 million olive trees. Though the tree is mighty tough and prepared to withstand severe hardship, it will fall short of its best unless the conditions include a moderate rainfall, light frosts and benevolent sun for three quarters of the year. The Spanish olive grower can do nothing about the weather but he can ensure that everything possible is done on the ground to nurture his trees and try to coax that delicate balance of all the natural resources to provide the best conditions for the crop to flourish in. So between harvests there is much work to be done: regulating the humidity of the soil, protecting the trees from weeds, pruning and ploughing to retain the rains of winter and spring. The latter is a highly skilled job for the expert only: dig deeper than 15 centimetres and the main roots could be damaged. It is vital to conserve all the moisture in the soil during the summer and then, in September, plough to trap the autumn rains, so important for maturation. The olives for oil are violet or blushing to violet when almost ripe, the best time to pick for the best oil. But harvest time in Spain, though it comes but once a year, varies by as much as three months depending on climatic conditions. In the more temperate provinces it is November, elsewhere January. Harvesting is a long, tedious and expensive business.

◀ Geographical distribution of olive tree cultivation in Spain

The method of gathering has changed little in thousands of years, not because Spanish olive growers are backward or unenterprising but simply because no better method has been discovered. Maybe there is something in the thought that the olive, proud and seemingly aware of its noble ancestry, resists change stubbornly, refuses to yield totally to science and progress.
Although mechanisation has been introduced by the olive oil industry in Spain for some of the processing, the machine capable of picking an olive from the tree without doing it irreparable harm has yet to be invented. Either its precious crop is hand picked or it will be forfeited. Hence the slow, costly, cumbersome but very necessary harvesting by manual methods. They vary but one of the commonest in Spain is threshing the branches with long poles, catching the fallen fruit in special sheets or nets on the ground. Another way is poetically and aptly known as milking, and that does really mean hand picking. The branches are caressingly combed with splayed fingers, the pickers working at ground level for the low branches and from ladders for the high ones.
The olive is quite unpredictable and even its experienced Spanish cultivators, who should know more about the olive and its moods than anyone anywhere, will never give thanks for a bumper harvest until every purpling fruit is safely in the mill. Which leads us naturally to the next stage, extraction.
The Spanish, current olive growing masters, would be the first to admit that their masters of the art were the Romans who should in turn give credit to their inspirers, the Egyptians. It is quite evident that the Romans were not simply producing superb roads and buildings for posterity; one of their less publicised achievements on the side, as it were, was the culture of the olive.
They perfected the methods of cultivation and extraction and the best tribute to their ingenuity is that the processes of extraction, preparation, grinding, pressing and separation (ie of water from the oil in the fruit) are essentially the same today. The Roman olive grower would recognise his methods in the Spanish mills of the 1970s,
where he would see the progeny, in the shape of a conical or cylindrical granite stone turning on a base millstone, of the grinding method he used 2500 years ago.
The production of olive oil is basically simple.
The art, the skill, the secret lies in the simplicity.
Thus, before the process begins, special storage containers

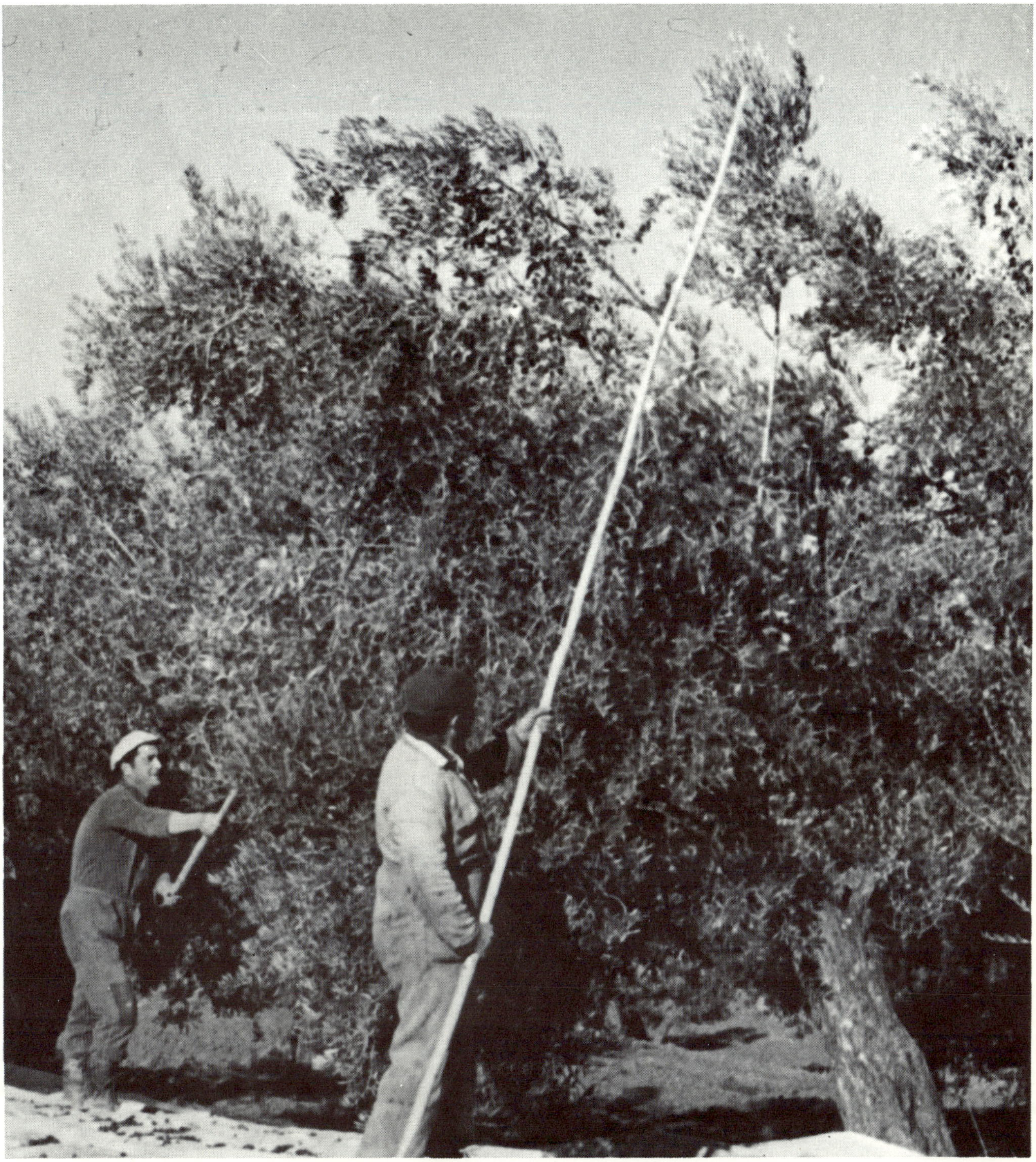

are used to prevent fermentation. The stores must be carefully
conditioned, so that ventilation and temperature are
controlled, and be scrupulously clean to avoid rancidity.
After weighing, selection and washing the olives are
conveyed to the crushing plant, where they are pulped.
The most important stage is then reached, the one where
modern Spain has the edge on Ancient Rome.
For the most modern equipment is used for the extraction
of the virgin oil or first pressing, by definition the finest
quality oil. But the olive yields more than one bounty,
for even after the best has been extracted the pulp still
contains good, usable oil. The remaining pulp is transferred to
hempen bags and these are crushed by hydraulic press to
draw off the surviving oil.
Spain is the world's largest exporter of olive oil and the
liquid gold finds its way into a hundred countries.
Exports have increased substantially in recent years
despite the fickle nature of the olive and the sharply
fluctuating harvest that can slump to a low of 200,000
metric tonnes after a bumper 650,000. Temperamental
and unpredictable the olive may be, diminutive in size
and not very handsome in appearance, what tree can
compare with it when it comes to universal reputation?
The oak fashioned the British Navy, stout furniture and
the hearts of England yet is still known only to a small
part of the world. The fir makes a marvellous telegraph
pole, the larch a powerful pit prop; the redwood is the
giant among trees, the maple yields syrup and the rubber
its sap and all benefit mankind to a varying degree.
But no tree in the world, fruit, wood or sap bearing, has the
versatility, the pedigree, the long, distinguished history,
the universality of the olive. The olive and its remarkable
fruit are part of the language and lore of all peoples everywhere.

15

It is unfortunately essential to know just a very little, very basic chemistry before it is possible to appreciate the value of olive oil in nutrition and medicine and the way in which it compares with other oils and fats. Under the heading of oils and fats, the first element of chemistry, albeit physical chemistry, is this: all normal vegetable and animal oils become solid fats if they are cooled enough and all fats become oils if they are heated enough.

The nature of fats and fatty acids Fats are formed when two sorts of compounds combine. One of these compounds is glycerine (glycerin, glycerol) and the other is an acid, a 'fatty acid' in this particular case. When compounds of this sort combine with one another the linking 'mechanism' is the spare 'bonds' that enable them to latch on to one another.
In a somewhat similar way the USA Apollo lunar module, after completing its mission and existing on its own, docks and latches on to the mother spacecraft.
The first of these compounds, the glycerine, has three spare bonds or attachment points and can therefore link with up to three of the other compounds, the fatty acids. True fats, which are the most abundant form of these compounds in nature, always have three fatty acids 'bonded' to a single molecule of glycerine, but compounds of 1 glycerine + 2 fatty acids (di-glycerides) and 1 glycerine + 1 fatty acid (mono-glycerides) do exist in nature and are also much used in the manufacture of foodstuffs for special purposes.
When the glycerine has its full complement of fatty acids (3) there is no room (or spare bonds) for any more. But this situation is not necessarily matched by the fatty acids each of which may have one, two, or many more spare bonds to start with. If a fatty acid has only one, that is used up in joining with the glycerine to become a 'saturated' fatty acid, it is 'full up' and has no capacity for further attachments. Fatty acids left, after combining with glycerine, with only one loose or spare bond are known as mono-unsaturated because they have only one remaining spare attachment. Yet others—the most important group—with several reactive points or bonds free even after firmly binding on to glycerine are known by the now familiar name of 'poly-unsaturates.

There are a great number of fatty acids of which it is only necessary to mention here the names of two: oleic, a mono-unsaturate, and linoleic, a poly-unsaturate.

Olive oil and digestibility Whether a fat is solid or an oil at normal room temperature depends on the individual fatty acids which are combined with the glycerine. Because olive oil contains a great deal of oleic and a modest proportion of linoleic, it is liquid at normal temperatures. This is an advantage in terms of digestibility, because oils and fats which are liquid at body temperature are obviously more easily handled by the body than those which remain solid.
The digestibility and absorbtion of olive oil has been studied for more than 60 years, in fact since the beginning of the era of rapid advance in the science of nutrition. As far back as 1910 it was shown that olive oil was superior in digestibility to sesame and peanut oil, and later (in 1936) that the absorbtion of olive oil was superior to that of other vegetable oils and very much superior to that of several animal fats.
There is no doubt whatever that in terms of straightforward nutrient value—and the basic value of a fat lies in the energy or calories it supplies—olive oil is certainly as good as any other and superior to most fats in digestibility and utilisation. But this knowledge in itself is not enough to provide reason to prefer olive oil to other edible oils in circumstances where an alternative is possible. A variety of other nutritional and medical factors must be considered quite apart from flavour, aroma and physical characteristics, in assessing olive oil for various purposes. Probably one of the most important of these considerations lies within the classification of fatty acids as saturated or unsaturated.

The significance of saturated and unsaturated
The terms 'saturated' and 'unsaturated', turned into plainer English, could be expressed as 'satisfied' and 'unsatisfied'. The 'satisfied' fatty acids have no loose bonds lying around; they are not able to grab other elements or chemical groups and therefore do not easily go rancid. Rancidity results when readily available atoms or molecules (such as oxygen) are picked up, either from the air or elsewhere.
On the other hand the unsaturated fatty acids—and linoleic in particular—are always vigorously on the

Nutrition, Diet and Health

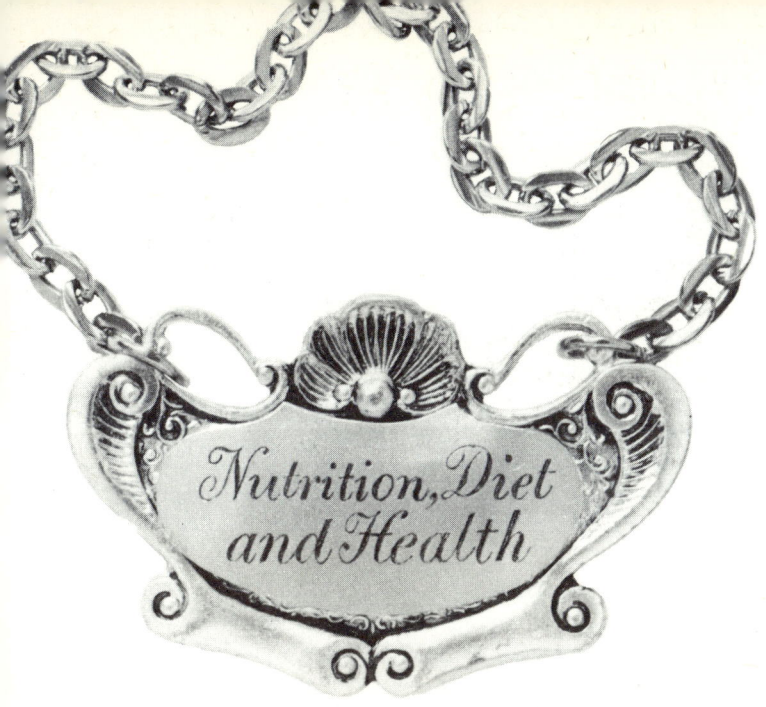

Dr R Gordon Booth, BSc, PhD, FRIC, MIBiol,
Fellow of the Royal Society of Medicine

lookout for free groups of atoms and molecules to which they could attach themselves and thereby become 'saturated' or satisfied.

The situation will now be slightly simplified for the sake of clarity because there are degrees of unsaturation, for example, mono-unsaturated or only *slightly* unsaturated fatty acids, and poly-unsaturated or *very* unsaturated and reactive fatty acids. For our purpose here we can lump together the saturated and mono-unsaturated fats and call them 'saturated' and call the poly-unsaturates just unsaturates.

It follows from this that saturated fats are for the most part very much more stable (un-reactive) than unsaturated fats. If this were the only consideration, the storage of foodstuffs containing fat would be a much simpler matter and the shelf life of the fat much longer, were the fatty acids involved all saturated.

Fats, vitamins and nutrition Now let us look briefly at some all-important nutritional facts. All fats serve as a source of energy or calories. They can be stored in various places in the body, beneath the skin, around the kidneys and elsewhere, where they have two functions as well as that of depot or reserve of energy:
they provide insulation and, where not carried to excess, have a cosmetic function.

Some fats are as important as vitamins, indeed if they were not energy sources and burnable by the body nor required in sizeable quantities, they would be classed as vitamins. The characteristic of an essential vitamin for humans is that it must be a substance or compound the body cannot produce, hence must be supplied ready-made in the food, otherwise health is seriously impaired.

The fats which function in this way are the unsaturateds and linoleic is the fatty acid without which the body eventually succumbs to a vitamin-like deficiency. (There are a few alternatives to linoleic, not so commonly found in nature, but we need not worry about them here). It has been determined experimentally that, on average, 6.5 g (ie nearly ¼ oz) of linoleic acid, ingested of course as a fat, is necessary per day for each individual. It is therefore obvious that in the foods consumed daily by the average individual there must be unsaturated as well as saturated fats, otherwise a nutritional deficiency will eventually occur. It is in this context that the composition of olive oil can be considered, particularly in relation to other oils and fats that form part of the diet, many just energy givers and lacking any essential components.

We can now consider the major component of all fats and oils, the tri-glycerides, forgetting for the moment other components like cholesterol.

As far as we know all saturated fats behave similarly in the body with the one possible exception of oleates, compounds of glycerin with oleic acid. It so happens that oleates are present in the great majority of natural fats and oils, usually in fairly substantial amounts.

The very widespread presence of oleates suggests that they may well have a function other than that of being merely a source of calories and stored fat. In the plant they are convertible into and are fore-runners or precursors of the essential unsaturated linoleic acid.

In the animal world there is evidence that oleates, together with linoleic and other unsaturated fatty acids, may be precursors or part precursors of the 'prostaglandins', the relatively newly discovered substances that regulate a number of things in the body such as blood pressure and metabolic rate. A lot of research on prostaglandins is going on and progress is so rapid it would be unwise to prognosticate, but they could become as important as hormones or antibiotics.

To revert to the well established and regular functions of saturated fats, it is clear that the nature of the fats consumed affects the nature of the fats stored in the body. Because olive oil consists mainly of low melting point (short-chain) fats and remains liquid at quite low temperatures, it affects storage or stored fat in this direction also, tending to make it softer and more plastic than would be the case if, for example, mutton fat were a large part of the diet. This is advantageous and implies (though conjectural at the moment) that such fat is more easily mobilised for disposal (to provide energy) than higher melting point fats.

When unsaturated fats are compared with saturateds, a very different nutritional picture emerges.

The vitamin hunt During the first third of this century many biochemists, physiologists and a relatively new kind of scientist, the nutritionist, experimentally fed a variety of animals, birds and insects on purified concentrated, diluted, unpurified and every other possible variant of food and food constitutent they could lay their hands on. This great vitamin hunt was started by Casimir Funk and Gowland Hopkins and joined later by scores of other investigators.

They observed that, in addition to the previously known nutrients—protein, fat, carbohydrate and minerals—accepted as normal, adequate components of foodstuffs, trace materials essential for health were to be found in a variety of natural foods but not, for example, in highly purified starch or sugar (carbohydrates) or very pure synthetic fats.

All this work on vitamins, made possible only by progressively improved scientific methods, inevitably led to more emphasis on the fundamental nutrients, protein, fat and carbohydrate. It was discovered in the 1920s that animals could not live without some fat in the diet once their body store of fats had been mobilised.

It is unnecessary to explain how this finding was refined into the certainty that for humans, saturated fats are non-essential (they can be produced from protein or carbohydrate in the body if necessary), but unsaturated fats vital because they cannot be synthesised by the body. As long as the body is provided with one suitable (eg linoleic) source of unsaturated fatty acid in its fat intake, it can make from this any others (eg linolenic, arachidonic) necessary.

It is therefore clear that unsaturated fats act like vitamins in that they are essential yet cannot be synthesised by the body; they are unlike vitamins because they are necessary in quantities of grammes per day instead of the usual vitamin requirement of milligrammes ($\frac{1}{1,000}$ g) or microgrammes ($\frac{1}{1,000,000}$ g), and supply a significant number of calories to the diet whereas vitamins supply none.

Olive oil and nutritional needs We should now consider the unsaturated fat content of olive oil in comparison with that of other fats and oils and relate it to physical needs and the physiological effects of too little or too much unsaturated fats in the diet.

Table 1 (page 20) gives the content of the principal edible vegetable oils of saturated and unsaturated fats.

Olive oil has an average 'unsaturated' content of about 10%. This has the sort of variation found in all natural biological materials, depending on the weather for the year, preceding harvest, the soil and the amount and proportions of soil nutrients available, and all the many

factors that affect crops the world over.
But this variability can be ignored in the light of all the other variables which arise in relating olive oil consumption to the need for unsaturated fatty acids and the undesirable results of taking too little—or too much— of them.
If olive oil were the only fat consumed our conclusions could be clearer but in various countries the proportion of olive oil in the total fat consumption varies considerably. In many Mediterranean countries, olive oil is the principal or one of the principal fats used both for direct consumption and in cooking, whereas in more Northerly countries solid fats (butter, margarine, lard) are preferred for many purposes. Furthermore, the higher the standard of living, the greater the proportion of animal fat consumed and even 'lean' meat contains a substantial proportion of fat, and eggs, milk and cheese also make their contribution.
These variations notwithstanding, to what extent does olive oil fit human nutritional needs? Here are the established facts and summarised international recommendations:

(1) Fat should be present in the diet in such amount as to provide 20-30% of total calories of the diet. (For a 3000 K-cal diet this means 60-100g of fat.)
(2) Assuming that (1) is met, then linoleic acid (the substantive part of unsaturated fat) is necessary in the proportion of 8-10% of total fat calories—for a 2700 k-cal diet this means 6-7 grammes a day.

Whereas in (1) fat *should* be present but saturated tri-glycerides need not, in (2) it is *essential* that the 6-7 g of the appropriate unsaturated fat be present.
Unsaturated fats, however, are not found in nature except in the presence of saturated ones and so to obtain unsaturateds one must also consume saturateds.
Looking back at the table of saturated v unsaturated components of natural oils and fats, we find that olive oil very neatly fits the requirements. If it is the only fat or oil consumed and constitutes 20-30% of the total calories, then it provides the normal requirement of linoleic acid. It is interesting to note in passing that human milk fat is very similar in composition to that of olive oil.
What happens in the absence of sufficient unsaturated fats or in the presence of amounts well above the normal requirement? The effects of shortage have been well

Table 1

Food	% saturated	% mono-unsaturated	% poly-unsaturated
1) Vegetable Oils			
Coconut oil	92	6	2
Olive oil	12	80	8
Palm oil (red)	45	45	10
Groundnut oil	18	56	26
Sesame oil	13	45	42
Soybean oil	14	30	56
Corn oil	16	27	57
Sunflower oil	10	18	72
Safflower seed oil	12	10	78
2) Solid Fats			
Butter	58	39	3
Margarine	64	30	6
Special margarine enriched with unsaturated acids	50	40	10
Shortening	24	67	9
Special shortening enriched with unsaturated fatty acids	26	61	13
Lard	32	54	14
3) Animal Fats			
Beef (American)	48	49	3
Veal	40	57	3
Lamb	40	55	5
Mutton	50	45	5
Pork	40	48	12
Farm-raised rabbits	40	44	16
Horse-meat	32	32	38
Chicken	26	50	24
Fish and shellfish	25		75
4) Miscellaneous			
Chicken eggs	31	53	16
Cocoa and chocolate	60	38	2
Mean composition of human fat	41	46	13

Frequently all classed together as 'saturated   Frequently referred to as 'unsaturated' explored though it is only recently that the necessity for some unsaturateds in the elaboration of prostaglandins has been established. Skin disease, stunting of growth and fatty infiltration of the liver are long established and well recognised symptoms of shortage.

An excess of unsaturated fats was established as a hazard very dramatically when their use in baby feeds produced acute anaemia resulting from the antagonism between vitamin E and poly-unsaturateds.

Excess of unsaturateds leads to an increased need for vitamin E. If there is no generous intake of vitamin E, excess unsaturateds can produce cirrhosis of the liver, anaemia and a variety of other conditions. So it becomes very obvious that, like many of the vitamins, an excess of unsaturateds can in certain circumstances be toxic whereas an inadequacy can lead to deficiency symptoms. By and large the message is clear: both excess and deficiency are harmful, the middle road is the safer and better one. As an individual item of diet, olive oil is firmly centred in the middle of the road.

Poly-unsaturates and heart disease Apart from their value in a vitamin-like role and as precursors of prostaglandins, the most publicised and controversial activity of poly-unsaturates is in connection with heart disease. The build-up in the aorta and medium sized arteries

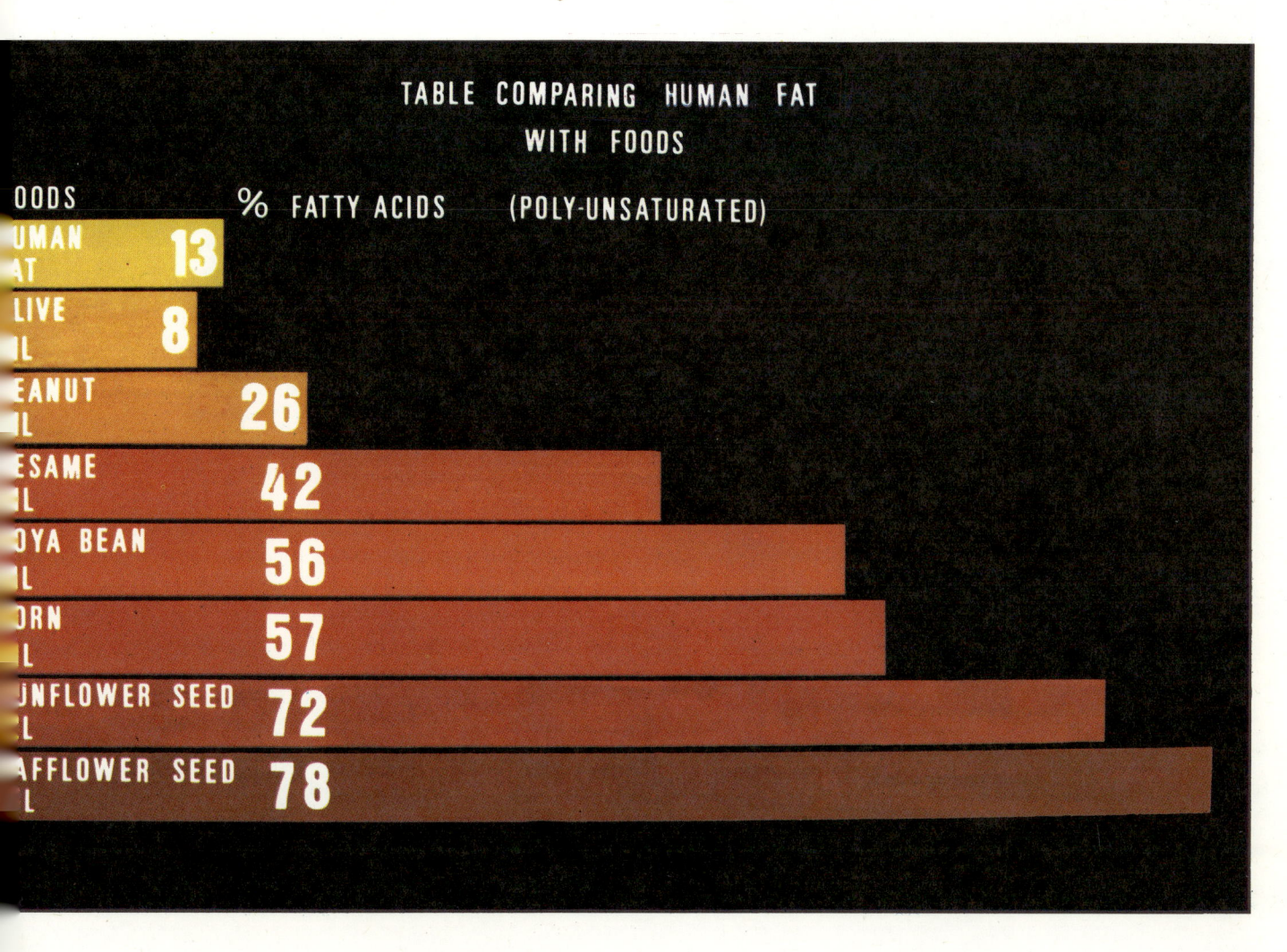

TABLE COMPARING HUMAN FAT WITH FOODS

FOODS	% FATTY ACIDS (POLY-UNSATURATED)
HUMAN FAT	13
OLIVE OIL	8
PEANUT OIL	26
SESAME OIL	42
SOYA BEAN OIL	56
CORN OIL	57
SUNFLOWER SEED OIL	72
SAFFLOWER SEED OIL	78

(including the coronary artery) of adhering 'flakes' or
granules known as atheromatous plaques, consisting of
cholesterol and a variety of other biological materials
which can lead eventually to coronary heart disease,
begins certainly no later than at age 20. The rate and
extent of this build-up, which can produce such severe
'furring up' of the artery as to cause a heart attack,
has been attributed to a number of causes, lack of adequate
poly-unsaturates leading to heightened blood serum
cholesterol being the most significant one.
Other causative factors put forward include stress,
excess sugar consumption, heightened serum tri-glyceride
(ie fat) levels, soft water drinking, smoking,
lack of exercise, genetic factors, among many others.
It would be fair to state that in the present state of
knowledge there is no known single cause and effect
relationship. All we can say with certainty is that the
change from a simple unsophisticated and relatively
primitive sort of diet to a rich one (say from rural
Greece to metropolitan America) means a corresponding
change in health rating from low risk to high risk.
It is a fact that consumption of adequate amounts of
poly-unsaturated fats normally leads to a reduction
in blood serum cholesterol levels and therefore can
reasonably be said to limit the rate of deposition of
plaques on the artery wall.
It is therefore wise to make sure that the diet contains
adequate amounts of poly-unsaturates and,
should this intake be very much in excess of normal
requirements, to consume plenty of vitamin E.
This broadly means that vegetable fats should be eaten
in preference to animal fats.
It is notable that populations which consume quite large
amounts of olive oil have a lower incidence of coronary
heart disease than those where a greater proportion of
animal fats and/or saturated, sometimes hydrogenated,
fats are eaten. While such a comparison, for instance,
between Greece and Finland, may be significant there
are too many other factors of difference involved to
make it in any way definitive.
In some quarters the presence or absence of cholesterol
in a fat or oil is regarded as important. It ought to be
pointed out that only a small proportion of the
cholesterol found in blood serum is derived from eaten
fats and oils; normally about 80% of it is synthesised in
the body. Therefore the presence or absence of cholesterol

in our food is of minor importance in this context.
It is, of course, true that cholesterol is a most important and very essential material within the body.
Among other things it is essential for the production of bile components without which fat digestion (and many other things) would go awry. The fact that olive oil, in common with many vegetable fats, contains very much less cholesterol than many animal fats is therefore of minor nutritional and medical significance.

The versatile oil We should now briefly consider the effect of frying or other cooking process on oils and fats. A recent and very detailed study has been carried out to establish what happens to animal and vegetable fats and oils customarily used for cooking. It was shown that olive oil, closely followed by lard, showed the greatest resistance to change on heating and aeration, whereas butter and sunflower seed oils showed the greatest changes. The recommendation made, on the basis of animal feeding trials, is that 'cooked' fat should be eaten as little as possible. Because the greater the initial unsaturation of the fat, the greater the production of peroxides and other undesirable materials, highly unsaturated fats are not recommended for cooking. If food must be fried, then olive oil is among the least affected and safest fats to use.

Olive oil has been used in medicine from time immemorial. Although advances in the range and efficacy of medicinal drugs and other materials during the past 50 years have been greater than all previous (materia medica) discoveries in the course of recorded history, there is nevertheless still scope for the use of olive oil.

In particular, stimulation of bile flow is easily and effectively accomplished by appropriate doses of olive oil, a treatment still used in hospital and private practice as it is also for some forms of constipation. Olive oil is also extensively used in the preparation of diets for those with very impaired digestions, especially the very young and the very old, where its exceptionally high digestibility makes it particularly valuable.

Finally a few points on obesity and its relation to fat intake. We have said an intake of unsaturated fat is essential for good health and that it does not exist in nature apart from saturated fat. Ideally about 25% of the calories in a diet should come from the fat consumed. Now it is obvious that true obesity is caused mainly by excessive deposition of fat in the normal storage areas. But this fat can have a carbohydrate or protein source, for the overall *calorie*, not fat, content of the diet is what counts. In fact, because fat is more satisfying than carbohydrate and not normally taken on its own (it's spread as butter or margarine or used in a dressing for salads) fat is less liable to be eaten in excess than the somewhat less satisfying protein and very much less satisfying carbohydrate. Furthermore, excess fat normally only accompanies general dietary excess (eg cream toppings on cakes). Indeed, one popular 'slimming' diet allows fats and proteins to be taken more or less ad lib but restricts carbohydrates, thus severely limiting the amount of fat which can be eaten.

So the specific limitation of fat intake *alone* as a means of countering obesity is non-productive. It is only valid, in fact only safe, when used as part of an overall food intake limitation, always bearing in mind the over-riding necessity for the vitamin-like unsaturated fats if good health is to be preserved.

Dr R Gordon Booth

Dr Booth is an international food consultant handling problems ranging from the design of wine and fruit juice plants to the development of medical and baby foods. His early academic studies were in agriculture and later biochemistry, specialising in vitamin and mineral aspects of human and animal nutrition.

He is a founder member of the Nutrition Society; member of the exclusive (37 members only) Association of Consulting Scientists; and on the Consultants Register of the Royal Institute of Chemistry, the British Institute of Management, and The Institute of Food Science and Technology.

Pre-War Dr. Booth was with the National Institute for Research in Dairying and Midland Counties Dairy, where he specialised in milk-based infant foods. He was then concerned with fish and fish oil research for British Cod Liver Oil Producers. During the war he worked, largely for the Ministry of Food, with the Cereals Research Station. After the war he joined Bovril Limited as Research Director and Chief Chemist and in 1951 moved to Petfoods Limited (Mars Group) as Research and Development Executive Director.

After spending nearly twelve years with Petfoods he established his own consultancy in 1962.

His clients have included Bayer, Courtaulds (very much concerned with the meat-like protein food 'Kesp'), Fisons, Gallagher, Heinz, Quaker Oats, United Biscuits, Youngs Seafoods, Milk Marketing Board, Pickerings Foods, Cadburys, Turkish State Planning Office, Financiera Prona SA and subsidiaries in Madrid, Murcia, and Burgos, Simmenthal SPA/Rome and Monza, and many other companies in the UK, USA and Europe.

25

Madame
Simone Prunier
introduces

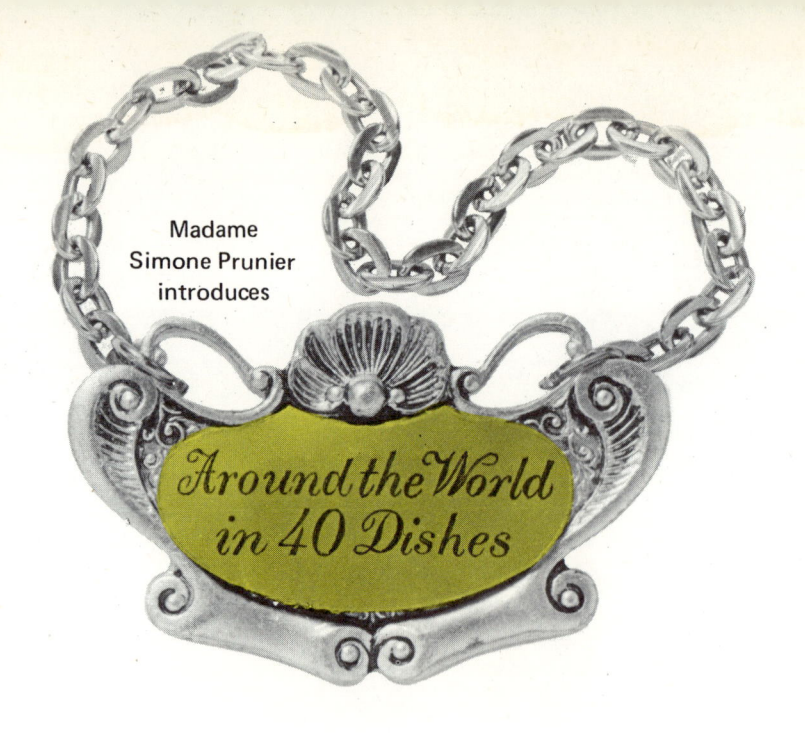

Around the World in 40 Dishes

I am delighted to introduce the international cooking section of this most interesting book. As a Frenchwoman with over 50 years' experience of the restaurant business I naturally realise the importance and versatility of olive oil. It is used all over the world in a great many classic recipes not only for cooking but also for sauces, salad dressings, mayonnaise and various kinds of canned fish.
Its fruity taste and resistance to rancidity make pure olive oil from those countries bordering the Mediterranean first choice for all who care about the culinary arts.
First a useful hint at the simplest level: the housewife who stores cans of sardines or tunny fish on her larder shelves would be well advised to leave them to mature
for several years. The difference in taste between canned fish left for that length of time and those eaten soon after purchase is quite considerable, believe me.
Olive oil has played an important part in the creation of classic dishes and sauces down the ages. Two of these, both well-known French recipes, are worth a closer look because they have a fascinating background and as I am interested in the origins of recipes, you will understand the historical allusions that follow.

26

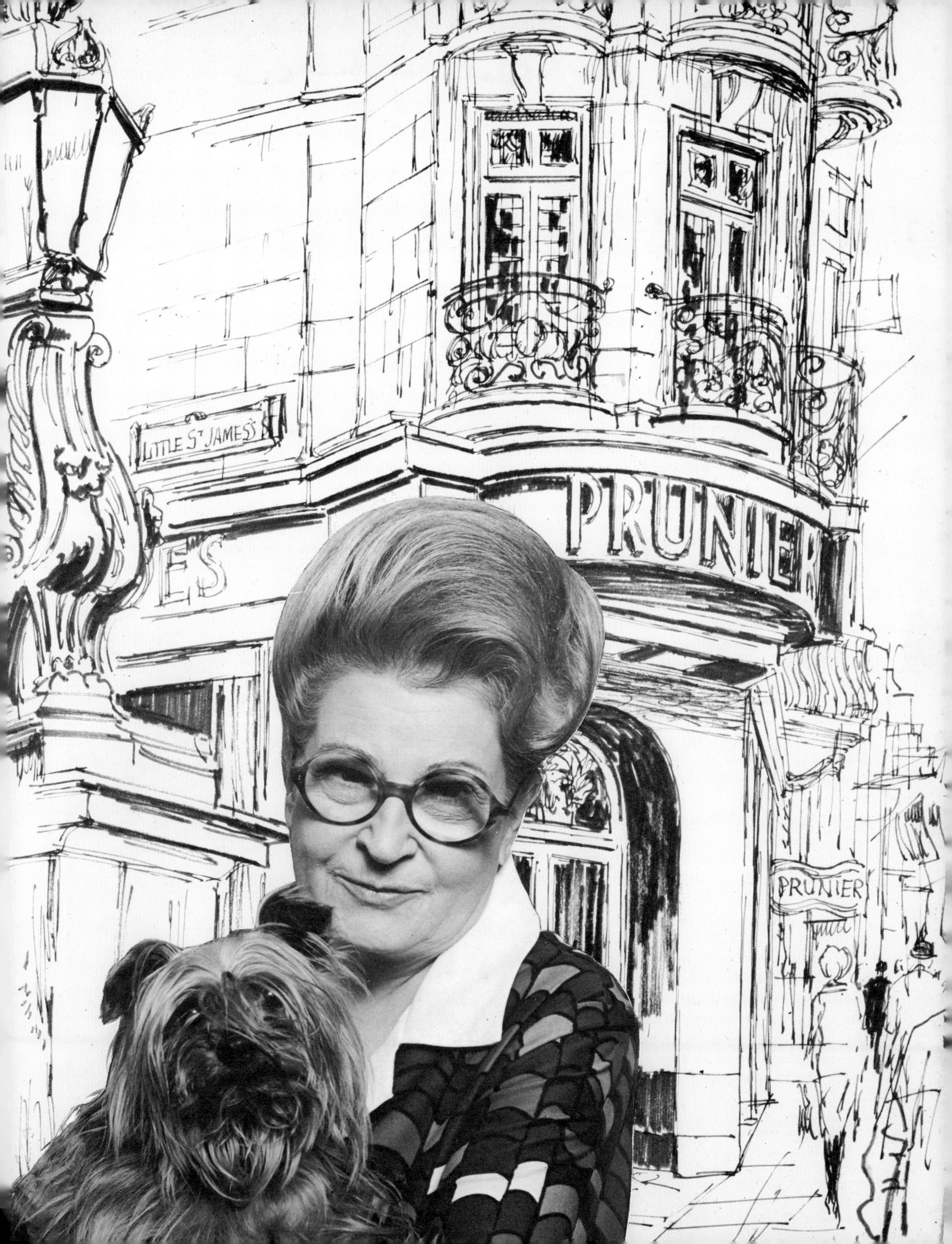
LITTLE S^T JAMES'S
PRUNIER
ES
PRUNIER

The two creations are Chicken Marengo and Mayonnaise. Legend has it that the first was conceived and served for the first time after the Battle of Marengo, Italy, at the turn of the 19th century. The chef of the future Emperor of France was obliged to produce a dish from ingredients available on the spot, the battlefield site. The principal items in Poulet Marengo — chicken, olive oil, eggs, olives, crayfish, tomatoes, mushrooms — make as popular a dish today as it was when Napolean ate it for the first time on the battlefield of Marengo 173 years ago.

The derivation of the term *Mayonnaise* has been the source of much argument in gastronomic circles for centuries. Some authorities say the word should be *mahonnaise* and Talleyrand's great chef, Careme, made a strong case for *magnonaise* from the French *manier* to stir (the eggs and oil). On the other hand, the Dictionnaire de l'Academic des Gastronomes says that the name derives from a source created on the spur of the moment by the chef of the Duc de Richelieu in 1756 to celebrate the master's conquest of Minorca (Balearic Islands) the capital of which is Port Mahon, hence *mahonnaise*.

Prosper Montagne accepts the alternative and more common word *mayonnaise* but not as a deformation of *moyennaise* from the old French word *moyen* (egg yolk).

Whatever its origins, mayonnaise is the name most people have given it for a long time. There may be doubt about the origin of the word but none at all about the need for the very best olive oil in the sauce's preparation.

The great Escoffier says that mayonnaise is used in most cold sauces and so may be regarded as a basic sauce just as Espagnole and Veloute are. It is simple to prepare but you have to bear certain things in mind. The idea that seasoning the yolks will cause separation is not shared by experts. On the contrary, it has been demonstrated scientifically that liquefied salt actually helps the eggs to bind the sauce. And because cold is the most likely cause of mayonnaise separating, it should never be prepared on ice.

In cold weather warm the oil a little or at least bring it to room temperature. The three causes of separation are basic mistakes in preparation: adding too much oil at the start, using oil that is too cold and too much in relation to the number of eggs.

Mayonnaise can be served with cold meats as well as cold fish, lobster, crawfish and crab; more unusually there is a mayonnaise for serving with sea urchins, mussels and truffles There is also a green mayonnaise made by simply adding three soup spoons of chervil, tarragon, watercress and burnet. Of the many other fascinating aspects of the olive and its oil, you can read elsewhere in this book.

To end my little personal contribution, it was interesting to discover recently an unusual use for olive oil which was quite unknown to me. Apparently it plays an intimate part in certain religious practices of the Roman Catholic Church where it is used, perfumed and blessed by a Bishop, as part of the anointing oil for Coronations, for the ceremonies of confirmation, ordination and baptism, as well as for blessing during the administration of the last rites. What a remarkably versatile product olive oil is!

But back, finally, to the main subject of this book and my principal interest: cooking. I leave you to browse through the catholic collection of recipes gathered from many countries of the world. Every one has been checked and approved by my chef. Remember that all need olive oil: don't spoil them by settling for any substitutes.

The good as well as the great dish deserves the best cooking medium. Bon appetit.

Madame Prunier

Madame Prunier was born in Paris, the granddaughter of Alfred Prunier, distinguished restaurateur and founder of the celebrated House of Prunier. Madame Prunier began her own long career as a restaurateur by working as her father's secretary and then learning the complex business of running a famous restaurant by actually getting involved with every aspect of its administration, from linen room to decoration, cashier's office to reception. She became a director of Maison Prunier in the late 20's and controlled the two Paris restaurants with her husband. She opened the London House of Prunier in 1935 and was managing director until 1952, when she became chairman additionally. Madame Prunier continued to play the dual role for another 20 years, finally relinquishing the chairmanship in 1972.
She remains director/consultant to Maison Prunier but still averages 12 hours a day in her office over the restaurant in St James's Street.
Madame Prunier has been and still is a member of various professional and commercial organisations in Britain and France. She was made a Conseiller du Commerce Exterieur in 1937 (one of the first women to be so honoured) and a Chevalier de la Legion d'Honneur in 1954. She is a member of the Hotel and Catering Trades Advisory Committee to the Department of Employment; honorary vice president of the Shellfish Association of Great Britain; a vice president of the Cookery and Food Association; and vice chairman of the Restaurateurs Association of Great Britain. Madame Prunier's son Claude is now President Directeur General of the two Restaurants Prunier in Paris, 9 Rue Duphot and the Traktir, 16 Avenue Victor Hugo, since his father has relinquished the function, though he remains actively associated on the same conditions as Madame Prunier. Her daughter Francoise is an artist.

CALDO VERDE A TERHEIRO (Portugal)

1 medium onion
3 pints water
1 teaspoon salt
3 potatoes, peeled and quartered
1 small white cabbage
½ cup Spanish olive oil
4 smoked sausages

Bring the onion to the boil in salted water, add potatoes and cook until soft. Strain vegetables and blend or push through a fine sieve back into their liquid. Wash cabbage and use enough of the heart to make about ½ lb of leaves. Shred them very finely and rinse again thoroughly. Add to the soup with oil and cook in an uncovered saucepan for about 5 minutes. Chop smoked sausages into small pieces about the size of a cork and heat through in soup just before serving.

SERVES 4 — 6

Each portion contains
240 Calories/18g carbohydrate
16g fat/6g protein
(based on a serving of 6 portions)

COURGETTES FARCIES (France)

8 baby marrows or courgettes
2 tablespoons Spanish olive oil
1 beaten egg
1 small onion, minced
4 tablespoons boiled rice
1 tablespoon grated Parmesan cheese
6 oz minced veal
2 oz minced ham
1 teaspoon oregano
1 crushed clove garlic
salt and black pepper

Poach courgettes whole for 1 minute in boiling salted water. Drain and cut off flower end. Halve carefully and scoop out the pulp: put in a bowl. Sauté onion in olive oil until transparent: add veal and ham. Mix all other ingredients into the marrow pulp and add to meat mixture. Stir over low heat for a few minutes, stirring all the time. Stuff marrow cases with this filling and place on an oiled baking tin. Bake at 375°F (190°C), Gas Mark 5, until tender — about 25 minutes. Allow two for each person.

SERVES 4

Each portion contains
245 Calories/10g carbohydrate
17g fat/13g protein

STARTERS

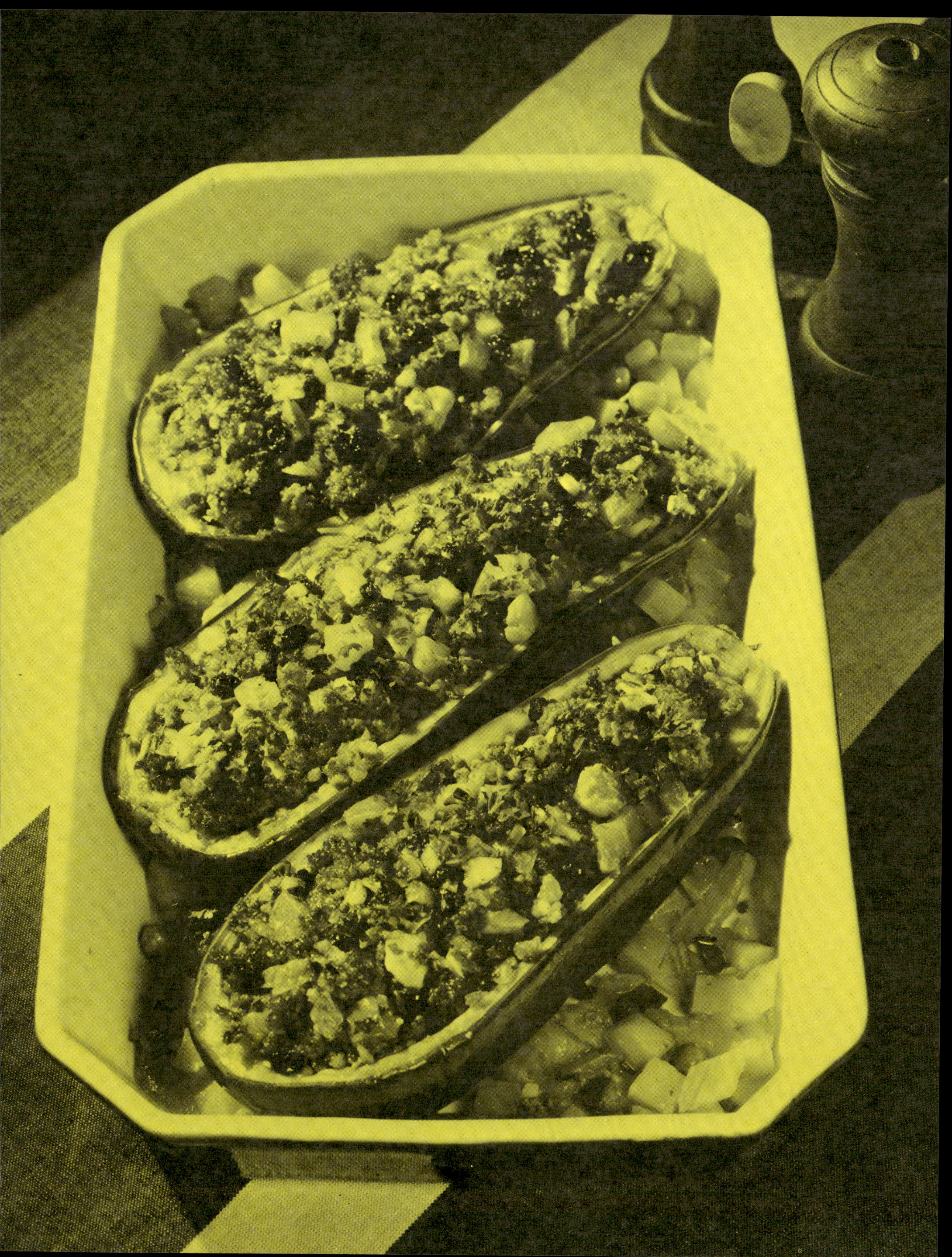

AVOCADO DIP (Barbados)

1 large ripe avocado pear
2 teaspoons fresh lime juice
2 teaspoons grated onions
4 tablespoons thick mayonnaise (qv)
dash of Tabasco sauce
dash of Worcester sauce
pinch of salt
paprika and chopped chives

Cut the avocado in half lengthways, remove stone but do not discard it. Scoop out the flesh and mash to a paste in the bowl. Add remaining ingredients and blend well, using a blender if you have one. Put the stone back into the mixture to prevent discoloration. Chill well.
Line a dish with crisp lettuce leaves, and pile in the mixture. Sticks of celery, raw carrots or potato crisps go well with this dip.

SERVES 2

Each portion contains
525 Calories/48g carbohydrate
51g fat/4g protein

BORTSCH (Russia)

1 large onion
1 leek
1 carrot
1 turnip
2 tablespoons Spanish olive oil
1 small cabbage (shredded)
4 tablespoons yoghurt or sour cream
1 large beetroot
stick of celery
1 quart stock or water and meat extract
bacon rinds
blade of mace
bunch of mixed herbs
a few carraway seeds

Fry chopped vegetables and bacon rinds in oil.
Boil beetroot in the stock for about an hour.
Remove; strain the stock and peel the beet. Slice into a pan and add the vegetables, drained of oil. Add all the herbs and season to taste with salt and pepper. Continue to simmer until all vegetables are cooked. Add a little grated nutmeg and remove mixed herbs. Serve very hot with a spoonful of sour cream in each plate.

SERVES 4 to 6

For 6, each portion contains
150 Calories/8g carbohydrate
12g fat/3g protein

33

SALSA GUASACACA (South America)

1 small onion (finely chopped)
2 tomatoes (chopped)
1 ripe avocado pear (peeled and diced)
1 small green pepper (diced)
2 hard boiled eggs (chopped)

dressing:

3 tablespoons Spanish olive oil
1 tablespoon white vinegar
¼ level teaspoon coriander
¼ teaspoon Tabasco Pepper Sauce
1 level tablespoon chopped parsley
salt and pepper

Place onion, tomatoes, avocado, green pepper and eggs in a basin. Mix together all ingredients for dressing and pour over avocado mixture. Mix gently until ingredients are well coated with dressing. Serve as a starter in individual dishes or glasses.

SERVES 4

Each portion contains
245 Calories/5g carbohydrate
25g fat/4g protein

MUSHROOMS MALAGA (Spain)

½ lb small button mushrooms
1 tablespoon lemon juice
2 tablespoons water
2 tablespoons white wine
2 tablespoons Spanish olive oil
1 tablespoon tomato purée
salt and pepper
parsley or chopped chives

Wash the mushrooms and trim stalks. Simmer water, oil, wine, lemon juice and a good sprig of parsley or chives together for 5 minutes. Add tomato purée, mushrooms and seasoning, cook slowly for a further 5 minutes and leave to cool. Serve cold as an hors d'oeuvre sprinkled with chopped parsley or chives.

SERVES 4

Each portion contains
135 Calories/31g carbohydrate
13g fat/3g protein

PIEROZKI (Poland)

5 oz dried or fresh mushrooms
4 tablespoons Spanish olive oil
4 oz chopped onion
1 egg
2 oz breadcrumbs
pepper and salt

for pastry:

1 lb flour
1 large egg made up to 3 fluid oz with cold water
pinch of salt

Wash mushrooms and leave to soak overnight if dried. Drain thoroughly. Mince onion and fry in oil. Mince the mushrooms and add to the egg, breadcrumbs and seasoning: pound to a pulp. Make the pastry and roll lightly; cut into small squares. Put spoonful of mushroom mixture into each square and make pierozkis by pressing the opposite ends together. Poach in boiling salted water until they float to the surface. Drain and serve with hot melted butter.

SERVES 4

Each portion contains
725 Calories/102g carbohydrate
29g fat/15g protein

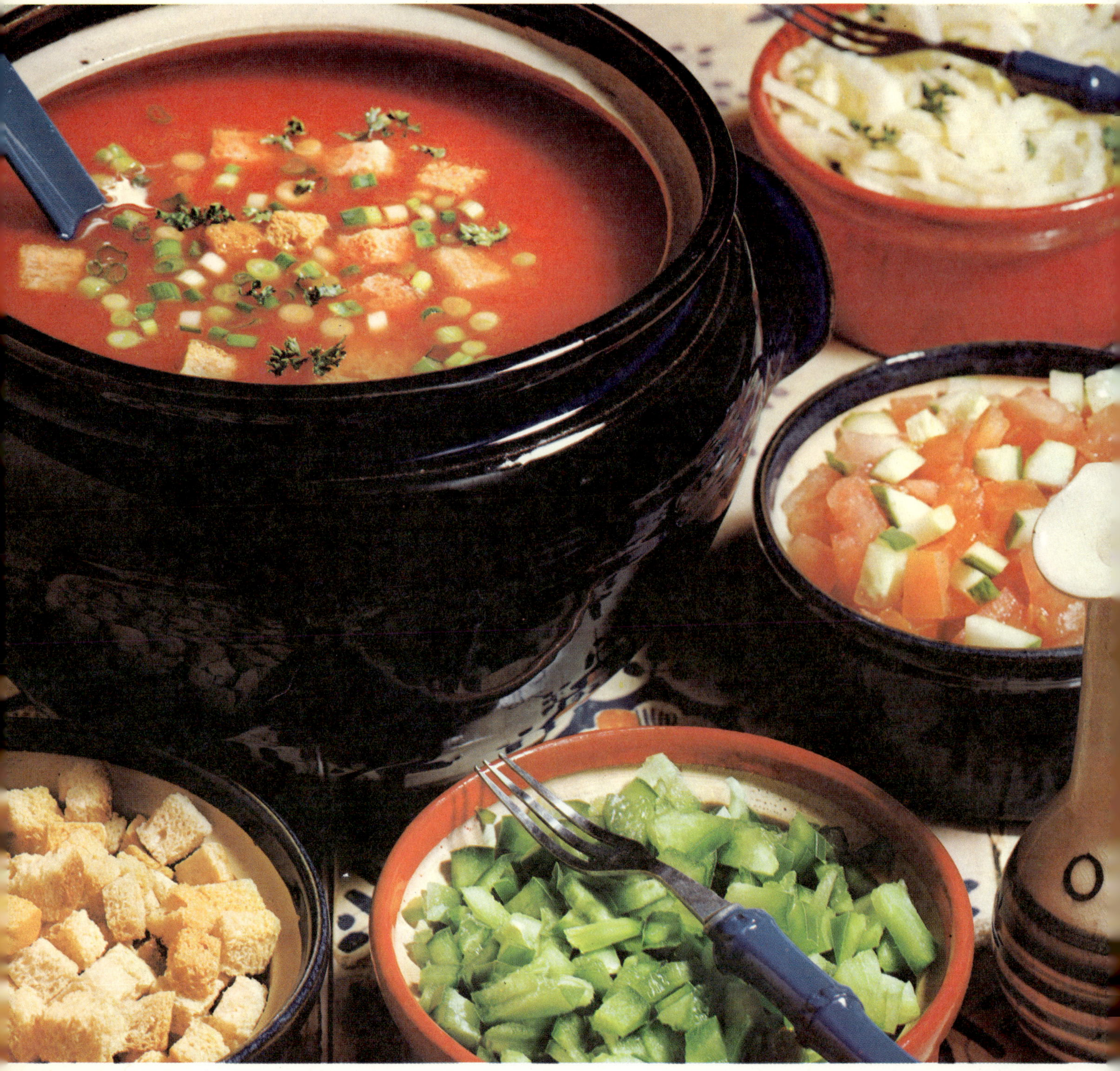

GAZPACHO (Spain)

1 lb ripe juicy tomatoes
1 onion
1 green pepper
1 clove garlic
3 tablespoons Spanish olive oil
¼ cucumber (peeled and cut into tiny cubes)
2 tablespoons wine vinegar
juice of 1 lemon
1 pint chicken stock
salt and ground black pepper

Skin and slice tomatoes. De-seed pepper and slice. Chop onion finely or put vegetables into a blender before mixing with the olive oil, vinegar and crushed garlic. Season to taste. Add chicken stock and lemon juice. Chill thoroughly and serve, preferably on ice, with diced cucumber and small cubes of toast.

SERVES 4

Each portion contains
195 Calories/5g carbohydrate
19g fat/2g protein
(Toast not included in calculation)

TARAMASALATA (Greece)

12 oz smoked cods roe
½ pint Spanish olive oil
juice of 1 lemon
1 teaspoon minced onion or garlic
freshly ground black pepper

Remove the outer skin from the roe and discard. Put the roe in a bowl and cover with 6 tablespoons olive oil. Leave for 10 minutes. Pound or mash the roe or it can be liquidised in a blender. Add the lemon juice. Beat in the remaining olive oil a little at a time. Mix in garlic or onion and the pepper. Pack into small pots and put in a cool place. Serve with toast as an appetizer garnished with parsley. Taramasalata can also be used as a savoury.

SERVES 4

Each portion contains
785 Calories/negligible carbohydrate
78g fat/21g protein

TOMATOES A LA GREQUE (Greece)

8 firm medium size tomatoes
2 tablespoons finely minced onion
1 tablespoon chopped chives
1 teaspoon chervil
1 teaspoon basil
pinch tarragon
1 clove garlic, crushed
1 tablespoon sultanas
finely chopped fresh parsley
½ pint French dressing (qv)

Skin tomatoes by immersing quickly in boiling water. Make three deep incisions across the tomato but do not cut through. With a small spoon remove seeds and core. Mix the onion and herbs with the dressing. Add the crushed clove of garlic and leave in a cool place for several hours. Plunge sultanas into boiling water and leave 5 minutes. Drain and add to onion mixture. Leave the tomatoes to drain in a dish in the refrigerator. Just before using, strain dressing, remove garlic. Fill the tomatoes with the stuffing and sprinkle fresh parsley across the top of incisions. Pour a little dressing over each tomato just before serving very cold. For an hors d'oeuvre allow two tomatoes for each person. They can be served on a crisp lettuce leaf or garnished with parsley.

SERVES 4

Each portion contains
365 Calories/35g carbohydrate
38g fat/trace only of protein

39

FISH DISHES

BOUILLABAISSE A LA PARISIENNE (France)

4 lbs fish (red mullet, rock salmon, turbot, John Dory,
　　crawfish, lobster are recommended but any firm fish
　　can be used as a substitute)
4 tablespoons Spanish olive oil
2 medium onions (chopped)
3 leeks (chopped white part only)
1 pint fish stock (made from bones simmered with a
bouquet garni)
½ bottle white wine
2 skinned and chopped tomatoes
a pinch of saffron
½ oz of crushed garlic
a bouquet garni

Fry lightly in olive oil the onions and leeks.
Moisten with fish stock and the wine. Add tomatoes, seasoning, garlic and *bouquet garni*. Bring to boil and boil for ten minutes. Add the firm-fleshed fish and lobster or crawfish which have been cut into slices across.
Then let the whole thing boil as hard as it can for a quarter of an hour. Meanwhile make a mixture of 3 parts of butter to 2 parts of flour and mash with a fork. Bind the soup with this and serve in a shallow dish surrounded with mussels or other opened shellfish. At the same time, serve in another dish some slices of bread, fried in olive oil, and soaked in the liquor of the bouillabaisse.

SERVES 6

Each portion contains
460 Calories/5g carbohydrate
29g fat/35g protein (excluding croutons)

ROUILLE (for serving with Bouillabaisse)

2 cloves of garlic
pinch of salt
2 oz anchovies, well drained
red mullet livers
1 large tin tomatoes
a little water

Sieve or crush with pestle and mortar the garlic and salt. Rinse the anchovies in hot water. Put the tomatoes in a saucepan with the water and keep over moderate heat until reduced by half. Allow to cool.

Make a further mixture of the following:

2 egg yolks
1 coffee spoon mustard
1 large teaspoon vinegar
add in
the mixture of garlic, anchovies and red mullet livers and tomato purée. Pour in drop by drop, in the same way as for mayonnaise, 2/3 tablespoons of Spanish olive oil (or more according to taste: the more oil, the richer and thicker the mayonnaise) until the mixture gets so firm that it detaches itself from the bowl. Test for taste and add pepper and salt if necessary. This is a very strong sauce and therefore one should serve one tablespoon per person to start with. The *rouille* gets softer and softer when it is kept but to keep it firm you can incorporate a large baked potato, mashed, in the original mixture. Serve it, apart from the Bouillabaisse, in a little sauce boat so that it can be served to the diner's taste.

Each portion contains
741 Calories/8g carbohydrate
70g fat/18g protein

RUSSIAN FISH PASTY

½ lb cooked and flaked cod, haddock
2 sliced raw mushrooms
1 onion (chopped)
2 tablespoons Spanish olive oil
1 beaten egg
4 oz boiled rice
1 tablespoon chopped parsley
salt and pepper
2 hard-boiled eggs
tomato sauce (accompaniment)
½ lb short pastry

Roll the pastry into a 10-inch square. Mix together the flaked fish, chopped mushrooms, rice and parsley.
Fry onion in olive oil until transparent but not brown.
Season mixture with salt and pepper; add onion.
Place half the mixture in the pastry, add sliced eggs and cover with the rest of mixture. Fold the two sides of the pastry together, one overlapping the other. Seal the two ends by moistening with milk and press firmly.
Brush with beaten egg and mark with a herring bone pattern along the centre to allow steam to escape.
Place on a greased dish and bake for 25 – 30 minutes at 400°F (200°C), Gas Mark 5. Serve with tomato sauce.

SERVES 4

Each portion contains
520 Calories/35g carbohydrate
34g fat/20g protein

TRUITE NICOISE (France)

4 fresh trout
8 oz tomato purée
4 tablespoons Spanish olive oil
clove of garlic
some anchovy fillets

Slowly fry the trout in olive oil. When almost cooked remove from heat. Mix tomato purée with a little olive oil and the crushed garlic. Line an ovenproof dish with this mixture and place the trout on top. Garnish the trout with the anchovy fillets and place in a warm oven for 20 minutes 325°F (170°C), Gas Mark 2-3.

SERVES 4
Each portion contains
320 Calories/39g carbohydrate
21g fat/29g protein

VALENCIA PANCAKES (Spain)

2 lbs fresh white fish (cod, haddock etc.)
2 lemons
2 tablespoons Spanish olive oil
1 oz flour
1 pint milk
4 oz mushrooms
1 tablespoon Madeira
salt and pepper
grated cheese
4 pancakes
flaked almonds

Boil the fish in salted water containing the juice of 2 lemons. When cooked, skin the fish, remove bones and flake. Make a sauce by heating the oil in a pan; stir in flour and gradually add hot milk. Add chopped mushrooms and wine. Simmer for 5 minutes and season to taste. Mix the fish into half the sauce. Make 4 fair-sized pancakes using the Enchillados recipe (qv). Fill each one with a quarter of the fish mixture and roll up gently. Place in a shallow ovenproof dish and cover with rest of sauce. Sprinkle with cheese and flaked almonds. Brown under the grill just before serving.

SERVES 4

Each portion contains
595 Calories/38g carbohydrate
34g fat/34g protein

BEEF STROGANOFF (Russia)

1 lb fillet or rump steak
2 tablespoons flour
1 teaspoon salt
2 onions
1 clove garlic
3 tablespoons Spanish olive oil
2 tablespoons flour (for sauce)
½ pint beef stock
1 tablespoon Worcester sauce
1 cup sour cream
parsley to garnish

Cut steak into thin 1-inch strips. Roll in flour and salt. Fry onions, garlic, mushrooms in oil for 5 minutes. Add steak. Brown well on all sides then remove meat mixture from pan and keep hot. To the oil in the pan add the flour, stock and Worcester sauce. Stir until thick. Pour in sour cream and simmer for 1 minute. Add meat and vegetables. Serve very hot, garnished with well-washed parsley and with plain boiled rice.

SERVES 4

Each portion contains
660 Calories/28g carbohydrate
48g fat/29g protein

CARIBBEAN KEBABS

for the marinade:

2 tablespoons Spanish olive oil
3 tablespoons rum
3 tablespoons soy sauce

for the skewers: (quantities shown are for each skewer)

2 2-inch cubes of veal
2 slices of green pepper
1 thick slice of banana
2 1-inch cubes of hard cheese (cheddar etc.)
1 pineapple chunk

Mix all marinade ingredients together. Add veal and leave for 2 hours, turning occasionally. Thread meat on to skewers and grill for 15 minutes. Push cheese, peppers, pineapple and banana on to the end of skewers and grill until cheese is golden and bubbly — about 2 minutes usually. Serve with fresh boiled rice.

SERVES 4

Each portion contains
110 Calories/3g carbohydrate
6g fat/4g protein

MEAT DISHES

CHILLI CON CARNE (Mexico)

1½ lbs minced lean beef
2 large onions, minced
1 can red kidney beans
1 medium can of tomatoes
1 teaspoon chilli powder
1 clove garlic, crushed
1 teaspoon salt
¼ level teaspoon pepper
mashed and creamed potato to garnish
chopped parsley and paprika to garnish
3 tablespoons Spanish olive oil

Heat the oil and fry the onion and garlic over gentle heat until soft but not brown. Add the meat and fry, stirring constantly. Combine beans, tomatoes and seasonings with chilli powder and add to meat mixture. Divide into four individual marmites or casseroles and top with a piping of mashed potato. Sprinkle with parsley and paprika and serve hot.

SERVES 4

Each portion contains
540 Calories/4g carbohydrate
41g fat/36g protein

46

GOULASH (Hungary)

1½ lbs stewing beef
2 large onions
2 tablespoons Spanish olive oil
2 carrots
1½ oz flour
1 tablespoon dried peas
3 tablespoons tomato purée
2 teaspoons paprika
1 pint boiling water
½ carton yoghurt
pepper and salt
bouquet garni
puff pastry to garnish

Prepare the meat and cut into cubes. Peel and chop onions and carrots. Sauté onion until golden then add meat. Slice carrots and add to pan with flour, paprika and tomato purée. Sir and cook for a few minutes. Add water, dried peas and seasoning to taste. Bring to boil and simmer gently for 2 hours. Half an hour before cooking ceases add the *bouquet garni.* When meat is ready remove herbs, turn into a fireproof casserole and keep hot. Roll out puff pastry: cut into half-moon shapes. Cook on a baking sheet in a very hot oven 425°F (230°C), Gas Mark 6. Before serving add yoghurt to casserole and top with pastry decorations.

SERVES 4

Each portion contains
445 Calories/20g carbohydrate
23g fat/13g protein
(excluding garnish)

MOUSSAKA (Rumania)

1 lb minced raw lamb
2 medium sized onions
3 aubergines
2 tablespoons tomato purée
¼ lb chopped button mushrooms
2 tablespoons Spanish olive oil
1 clove garlic
salt and pepper
parsley

for the sauce:
1 oz flour
2 tablespoons Spanish olive oil
¾ pint of milk
4 oz grated cheese

Fry minced onion in the oil. Add meat, mushrooms and one aubergine cut into thick slices. Chop garlic finely and add with salt and pepper and tomato purée.
Cut the remaining aubergines into ½-inch slices and line an ovenproof dish with them, having oiled it well previously. Pile the meat mixture into the centre and cover with the sauce made as follows:
Put oil in a pan, add flour and cook for 2 minutes. Stir in milk gradually away from heat. As it thickens replace over low heat and add 3 oz of grated cheese. Pour sauce over meat mixture and cook in a very moderate oven, 325°F (170°C),
Gas Mark 3, for approximately 1½ hours.
Sprinkle the rest of the cheese on top and brown under the grill. Sprinkle with fresh chopped parsley before serving.

SERVES 4

Each portion contains
985 Calories/15g carbohydrate
83g fat/35g protein

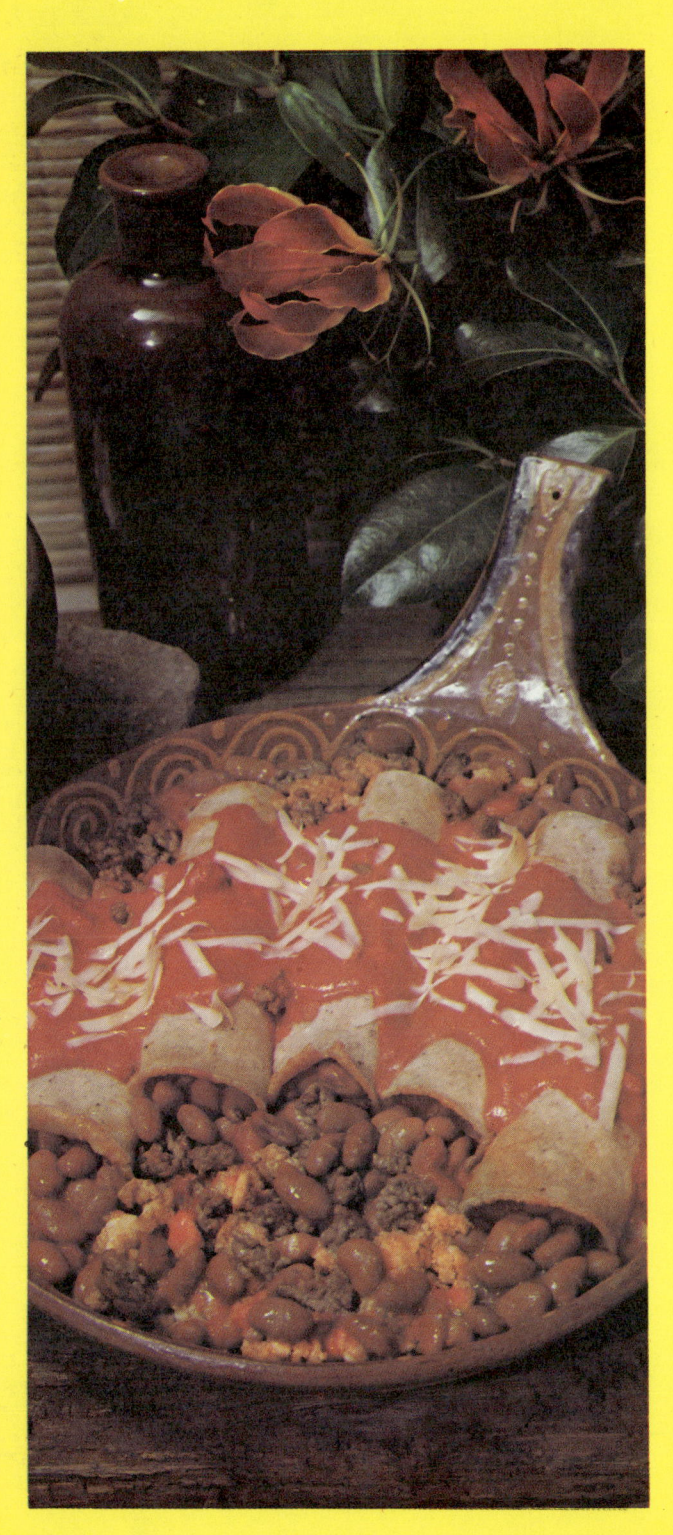

ENCHILLADOS (Mexico)

for the pancakes:
3 tablespoons flour
1½ tablespoons cornflour
7½ fluid ounces water
1½ tablespoons Spanish olive oil

For the filling:
1 medium sized onion
2 tablespoons Spanish olive oil
1 lb minced beef
1 can red kidney beans
1 teaspoon chilli powder
pepper and salt
½ pint thick tomato sauce
2 oz grated cheese

Make the batter and leave to stand for 30 minutes in a cool place. Make the filling by chopping onion and frying gently in oil. Stir in the meat, chilli powder, pepper, salt and beans. Heat until brown. Prepare the pancakes by lightly oiling a thick pan and pouring in a good tablespoon of the batter, allowing it to run all over the pan in a thin coat. Leave until dry but not brown. Make eight small, thin pancakes and put on one side. Fill each one with the meat filling and roll up.
Place in a fireproof dish, cover with tomato sauce and reheat in a hot oven for a few minutes. Sprinkle with grated cheese before serving.

SERVES 4

Each pancake contains
375 Calories/27g carbohydrate
21g fat/20g protein

PEPPERPOT PORK (West Indies)

1 lb lean pork in 1-inch cubes
2 green peppers
1 red pepper
1 egg
2 tablespoons flour
½ teaspoon salt
½ teaspoon pepper
1 chicken bouillon cube
½ cup pineapple juice
2½ tablespoons cornflour
2½ tablespoons soy sauce
½ cup soft brown sugar
½ cup vinegar
2 tablespoons Spanish olive oil

Remove seeds from green peppers and cut into slices. Boil for about 7 minutes; drain. Mix soy sauce, vinegar, pineapple juice and soak pork in the marinade for about 2 hours, turning frequently. Make a batter of egg, flour, salt and pepper. Drain pork cubes, dip in batter and fry in hot oil until golden. Drain off excess fat. Make ½ pint chicken bouillon and pour half the quantity into the pan. Add the drained marinade, sugar and the rest of the bouillon mixed with the cornflour. Heat, stirring all the time until the sauce thickens and clears. Add peppers and pork cubes. Serve with hot boiled rice.

SERVES 4

Each portion contains
680 Calories/44g carbohydrate
41g fat/33g protein

PORK CHOP SUEY (China)

½ lb lean pork, shredded
¾ lb bamboo shoots
1 can bean sprouts
1 oz vermicelli (soaked for 15 mins)
1 teaspoon salt
8 tablespoons Spanish olive oil
5 dried mushrooms (soaked for 3 hours in water)
½ lb spring onions
3 tablespoons soy sauce
1 tablespoon wine or sherry
good pinch monosodium glutamate

Heat half the oil and fry shredded meat and sliced onions. Heat remaining oil and fry other vegetables and vermicelli. Mix meat, vegetables and fried vermicelli together and add seasonings, soy sauce and wine or sherry. Serve very hot with noodles.

SERVES 4

Each portion contains
670 Calories/44g carbohydrate
54g fat/11g protein

PORK AND RED CABBAGE CASSEROLE (Austria)

1 lb lean pork loin (boned)
I small hard red cabbage
2 medium sized onions
2 cooking apples
2 tablespoons Spanish olive oil
2 tablespoons sugar
2 tablespoons wine or dry cider
2 tablespoons wine vinegar
bay leaf
bouquet garni
pepper and salt

Trim fat from loin and cut into small pieces of about 2 inches. Marinade in oil and wine vinegar, turning occasionally. Trim cabbage by removing outer leaves and stalk. Shred the remainder thinly and wash well in salted water. Have ready an earthenware or fireproof casserole. Put in layers of cabbage, sliced onion, and peeled, cored and sliced apples and herbs. Pack well down and cover with liquid to which you have added the sugar and seasoning. Cover closely and cook slowly in the oven for about 3 hours 325°F (170°C), Gas Mark 2.

SERVES 4

Each portion contains
555 Calories/31g carbohydrate
35g fat/29g protein

STUFFED PORK POLONAISE (Poland)

1½ lb of lean pork steak
2 tablespoons Spanish olive oil
1 oz mushrooms
1 oz flour
1 oz capers
salt

For the stuffing:

6 oz calves or pigs liver
2 oz lean bacon
4 oz onion
2 tablespoons Spanish olive oil
1 egg
1 oz breadcrumbs
pepper and salt

Pound meat into a thin collop. Mince stuffing ingredients and mix together. Salt, and spread stuffing evenly over meat. Roll up and tie carefully. Place in a roasting tin with the oil and 2 tablespoons water. Baste frequently for 30 minutes at 350°F (180°C), Gas Mark 3. Add mushrooms and capers and cook for another 30 minutes. Untie and discard string before serving on a hot dish in its own liquor.

SERVES 4

Each portion contains
575 Calories/8g carbohydrate
37g fat/50g protein

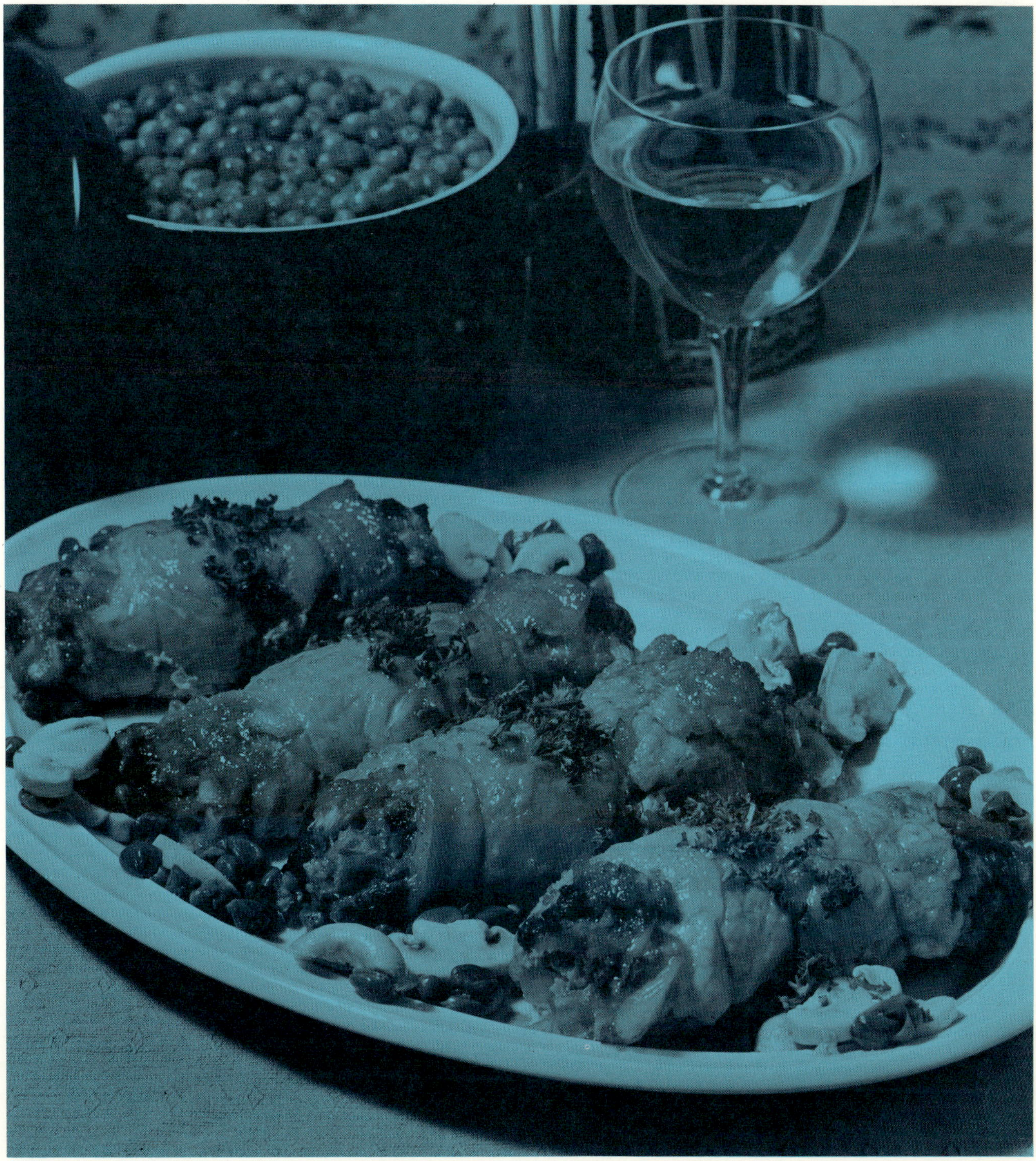

SUKIYAKI (Japan)

1½ lbs rump steak cut into thin strips
2 tablespoons Spanish olive oil
¼ cup water
1 green pepper
½ lb mushrooms
¼ cup sugar
¾ cup soy sauce
2 medium onions
1 can bamboo shoots
6 spring onions
sake or sherry (2 tablespoons)

Heat oil in a frying pan, add meat and brown, turning all the time. Mix sugar, soy sauce and water together. Pour half this mixture over the meat: cook 1 minute. Place meat at side of pan; add onions and green pepper. Cook 2 to 3 minutes then add sliced bamboo shoots and mushrooms. Cook 3 to 5 minutes. Chop spring onions, including the green stalk. Put in pan with the rest of the sauce and cook for 1 minute: pour in the sake or sherry. Bring to boil and serve with hot boiled rice.

SERVES 4 — 6

Each portion contains
323 Calories/9g carbohydrate
21g fat/25g protein
(Based on 6 portions excluding rice)

SWEET AND SOUR PORK (China)

1 lb pork
1 tablespoon sherry
2 tablespoons soy sauce
2 tablespoons flour
1 tablespoon cornflour
Spanish olive oil for frying (approx 4 tablespoons)
1 green pepper
1 medium size onion
1 carrot (parboiled for 6 minutes)
1 small bamboo shoot, sliced
2 slices pineapple (optional)
5 tablespoons Spanish olive oil

Sauce:

4 tablespoons sugar
2 tablespoons soy sauce
1 tablespoon cornstarch
½ cup cold water
1 wineglass wine vinegar
4 tablespoons tomato sauce

Cut pork into 1-inch cubes and mix with sherry, soy sauce, flour and cornflour. Fry meat in hot olive oil until crisp and golden brown. Put into a dish. De-seed and dice green pepper. Slice onion and carrot, add to bamboo shoot and pineapple (diced). Heat 5 tablespoons olive oil and sauté vegetables for 5 minutes. Mix all the sauce ingredients together and add to sauté mixture. Bring to the boil, stirring all the time. If too thick add a little strained pineapple juice to the pan.

SERVES 4

Each portion contains
755 Calories/56g carbohydrate
49g fat/27g protein

53

VEAL ST LUCIA (West Indies)

4 veal chops
3 tablespoons Spanish olive oil
1 wineglass white wine
4 tablespoons peanut butter
4 shallots
1 clove garlic
1 red pepper
tomatoes, mushrooms to garnish

Paint veal chops with peanut butter and leave for 1 hour. Fry in oil and remove from pan. Add sliced garlic and shallots to pan juices. Sauté lightly until transparent. Add white wine and sliced, seeded red pepper.
Put in chops and cook slowly for about 20 minutes, turning once. Serve with a green salad to which a few pineapple cubes have been added.

SERVES 4

Each portion contains
550 Calories/14g carbohydrate
34g fat/45g protein

55

POULTRY

CHERRY BLOSSOM CHICKEN (Japan)

½ lb raw chicken
¼ lb mushrooms
1 onion
1½ tablespoons Spanish olive oil
1 teaspoon salt
4 tablespoons chicken stock
3 eggs
3 tablespoons sherry or sake
4 tablespoons sugar
3 tablespoons soy sauce
½ lb fresh peas
a little spinach (approx 4 oz cooked)

Chop chicken, mushrooms and onion into small pieces. Boil peas. Wash spinach well and cut into thin strips. Fry mushrooms and onions in oil: then add sake or sherry, sugar, salt and soy sauce. When hot add chicken pieces. Cover with a lid and stand over boiling water or turn into another heatproof dish and place in a steamer. Keep over a medium flame and when the liquid decreases add peas and spinach. Beat the eggs and spread over the top. When the eggs are solid, remove from heat.
This dish is delicious cut into wedges and served like a pie with green salad.

SERVES 4

Each portion contains
385 Calories/38g carbohydrate
16g fat/22g protein

CHICKEN LAHORE (India)

1 chicken (about 3 lbs)
1 medium onion, finely chopped
2 tablespoons Spanish olive oil (+ 1 tablespoon later)
½ teaspoon coriander
2 tomatoes, pulped
1 crushed clove garlic
pinch of saffron
1 teaspoon ginger, finely chopped
½ teaspoon turmeric
juice of half a lemon and a sliver of the peel

Wash and wipe the chicken. Put all the other ingredients into a large bowl and mix well. Put the bird in this spicy marinade and leave for about 3 hours, basting frequently. Put a large piece of foil in a baking tin or large casserole. Place the chicken on it and pour over the marinade making sure that it is evenly distributed over the bird. Add 1 more tablespoon of oil and then cover and seal the foil. Cook in a moderate to hot oven, 375°F (190°C), Gas Mark 5. Put the chicken on a dish with its juice and serve with plain boiled rice.

SERVES 4

Each portion contains
490 Calories/trace carbohydrate
35g fat/43g protein

57

CHICKEN MANDARIN (China)

4 chicken joints
1 small bamboo shoot
1 leek
4 slices ginger
6 tablespoons Spanish olive oil
2 tablespoons rice wine or sherry
8 tablespoons soy sauce
2 cups chicken stock
1 teaspoon sugar
3 tablespoons green peas
pinch monosodium glutamate

Cut bamboo shoot and leek into slices about 1-inch thick. Heat oil in pan and fry leek and ginger for a few minutes. Add chicken and bamboo shoot and continue to fry. When chicken stiffens and browns add wine and soy sauce. Add sufficient stock to cover the chicken. Cook over moderate flame for about 20 minutes according to size of joints. Add sugar and keep over low flame for another 30 minutes. Add peas and monosodium glutamate. Cook for a further 5 minutes and serve hot with rice.

SERVES 4

Each portion contains
595 Calories/65g carbohydrate
49g fat/10g protein

CHICKEN MARYLAND (United States)

1 very young capon
1 egg
dried breadcrumbs (2 oz or more)
½ pint Spanish olive oil
salt and pepper

Cut capon into pieces for serving. Dip the pieces into beaten egg and then into breadcrumbs seasoned with salt and pepper. Quickly brown the chicken in boiling olive oil and then cover pan and cook very slowly for 30 minutes turning occasionally. Drain on kitchen paper before serving. The usual accompaniment for this dish is corn fritters and fried banana; sometimes crisp bacon rolls and tomatoes are used as a garnish.

Corn Fritters

1 tin sweetcorn
2 eggs
breadcrumbs from one small white loaf
salt and pepper
8 tablespoons Spanish olive oil

Beat eggs. Add corn (drained of liquid) salt, pepper and breadcrumbs to bind the mixture. Shape into flat cakes and fry in olive oil until golden brown.

SERVES 4
Each portion contains
570 Calories/72g carbohydrate
120g fat/50g protein

BIBER DOLMAS AND YALANCI DOLMAS (Turkey)

4 large green peppers
cabbage leaves (raw)
10 oz rice
4 oz sultanas
1 large chopped onion
½ pint stock
1 — 2 tablespoons Spanish olive oil

Slice the top of the peppers and remove core and seeds. Mix rice, onion, sultanas and a little olive oil together. Stuff the peppers with this uncooked mixture leaving space for the rice to expand. Wash the cabbage leaves in cold salty water. Wrap the rest of the mixture in the leaves. Pour stock into a fireproof dish and place the peppers and cabbage leaves in the stock. Season with salt and pepper and cook in a medium oven 350°F (180°C), Gas Mark 4, until vegetables are soft. Dolmas are best served cold but to make an appetizing hot dish add 4 oz minced lamb to the stuffing mixture. Thicken the stock in which the dolmas have cooked for a savoury sauce.

SERVES 4

Each portion contains
320 Calories/93g carbohydrate
5g fat/8g protein

GARLIC EGGS (France)

4 cloves garlic
2 anchovy fillets
1 tablespoon capers
6 hardboiled eggs
3 tablespoons Spanish olive oil
1 tablespoon wine vinegar
salt and pepper to taste
chopped parsley

Chop and crush garlic. Add the anchovies and capers and pound together to make a paste. Blend in oil, vinegar, salt and pepper. Shell the eggs; cut into quarters and cover with the sauce. Sprinkle with parsley.

SERVES 4

Each portion contains
295 Calories/0g carbohydrate
29g fat/9g protein

RICE AND EGG DISHES

RISOTTO (Italy)

1 oz butter
2 wineglasses dry white wine
1 red pepper (de-seeded and chopped)
4 oz cooked peas
2 tablespoons Spanish olive oil
1 large onion
12 oz Italian rice
2 pints chicken stock
6 mushrooms
4 oz cooked ham (or minced beef previously browned in olive oil)
Parmesan cheese

Heat oil in pan, add sliced onion and cook until soft. Add rice, stir until translucent then pour in wine and cook until almost evaporated. Pour half the stock and chopped red pepper into pan. Cook uncovered until the rice is nearly dry but not sticking. Add remaining stock and continue to cook until rice is ready. Fry mushrooms in a little oil and chop. Stir the rice frequently and when ready put in diced ham and peas. Add butter and diced mushrooms. Sprinkle with Parmesan cheese just before serving.

SERVES 4

Each portion contains
510 Calories/66g carbohydrate
19g fat/8g protein

62

SPANISH RICE

6 tablespoons Spanish olive oil
2 tablespoons lemon juice
1 crushed clove garlic
1 teaspoon mustard
6 oz long grain rice, cooked
3 tablespoons cooked peas
3 tablespoons spring onions, chopped
1 tablespoon stuffed green olives
1 tablespoon black olives
2 large firm tomatoes
2 tablespoons diced cucumber
2 tablespoons sultanas (boiled in a little water
for 5 minutes)
pepper

Mix oil, lemon juice, garlic and seasonings together.
Put all the other ingredients, including the strained sultanas, into a bowl and pour dressing over. Stir well and leave in a cool place.

SERVES 8 Halve the quantities for four people.

Each portion contains
225 Calories/12g carbohydrate
20g fat/trace protein

TOMATO OMELETTE (France)

4 ripe tomatoes
2 tablespoons Spanish olive oil
6 eggs
pinch of basil
salt and pepper
parsley to garnish

Dip tomatoes in boiling water to remove skins. Take out the seeds and cut up tomato flesh into pieces. Fry slowly in olive oil for 5 minutes. Allow to cool. Beat eggs.
Add the tomato mixture, basil and seasonings. Melt an ounce of butter in a thick frying pan. When sizzling pour in egg mixture. As it thickens lift at the edges with a fork until nearly all the liquid has disappeared. Loosen the edge of the omelette at one side with a spatula.
Fold over quickly and turn upside down on a hot plate. Garnish with parsley.

SERVES 2 Repeat for four servings

Each portion contains
480 Calories/trace carbohydrate
44g fat/19g protein

SALADS AND VEGETABLES

INSALATA OLIVES (Italy)

½ lb stoned green olives
½ lb stoned black olives
1 green pepper
1 red pepper
¼ teaspoon oregano
4 tablespoons Spanish olive oil
juice of 1 lemon
1 sweet onion
salt and pepper
lettuce leaves

Core peppers, de-seed and cut into thin strips. Mix all ingredients together and add pepper and salt to taste. Keep very cold for at least an hour. Line a dish with crisp lettuce leaves. Pour in olive salad and decorate with onion rings. The addition of quartered hard-boiled eggs makes this salad an appetizing meal.

SERVES 4

Each portion contains
350 Calories/11g carbohydrate
37g fat/12g protein

MEXICAN SALAD

1 lb cooked fresh haddock
½ lb tomatoes, peeled and chopped
4 oz cucumber, peeled and diced
1 green pepper, seeded and sliced
2 tablespoons Spanish olive oil
1 tablespoon wine vinegar
2 hard boiled eggs (for garnishing salad)
chopped onion and parsley
watercress
radishes
lettuce leaves

Flake the fish, season with salt and pepper and mix with the tomato, cucumber and pepper. Make a dressing by blending the oil and vinegar together with finely chopped raw onion and parsley to taste. Pour over the salad and toss well. Serve on a bed of lettuce garnished with watercress and radish roses and eggs.

SERVES 4

Each portion contains
275 Calories/2g carbohydrate
17g fat/29g protein

PORTUGUESE SALAD

8 oz flaked, cooked crabmeat
8 oz cooked, shelled prawns
12 oz cooked, diced lobster meat
12 oz cooked flaked turbot or halibut

for the dressing:
½ pint Spanish olive oil
6 tablespoons each chopped parsley and chives
1 tablespoon chopped fresh tarragon
1 lettuce
bunch of watercress
4 skinned tomatoes
8 black olives
8 green olives

Prepare all the fish and put into a bowl. Mix together oil and herbs and pour 2 — 3 tablespoons over the fish. Place in the refrigerator to marinade for about 2 hours. Just before serving prepare lettuce and watercress and cut tomatoes into quarters. Toss lightly in remaining dressing and arrange on a large shallow dish. Pile the fish into the centre and garnish with olives.
Pour any remaining dressing over the salad before serving.

SERVES 4

Each portion contains
1000 Calories/2g carbohydrate
85g fat/56g protein

Home Cooking with Olive Oil

Marguerite Patten

I have spent many years writing and talking about home cooking and I think this has given me a good insight into the kind of foods and dishes enjoyed by the average family. Most people require well-cooked, interesting and varied meals, that are not too difficult, expensive or time-consuming to prepare. The recipes I have chosen for this section of the book will, I hope, meet with these requirements. At the same time they give an idea of some of the practical uses of olive oil in cooking.
Olive oil is one of the most valuable and versatile commodities to use in cooking. As I am sure you realise, it has been used by good cooks of all countries for centuries. The modern Spanish olive oil of today is refined and very pure but it is just as adaptable and valued as the oil of older times.
I would like to outline some of the many ways in which I use Spanish olive oil. Firstly it is a perfect ingredient in which to fry foods—whether sweet (such as fritters or doughnuts) or savoury (as our well-liked fish and chips).

Frying is not the easiest method of cooking—you must achieve a sufficiently high temperature to 'seal in' the flavour of the food and prevent it being greasy and unappetising. Olive oil has the great advantage that it can be brought to a sufficiently high temperature for perfect frying without fear of over-heating, which would happen with other kinds of fat. It is so easy to pour out just the right amount of oil from the bottle when shallow frying, or to use the oil over and over again when deep frying, so olive oil is economical for frying as well as being so efficient. Later we give the secrets of successful frying, which I hope you will find helpful.

Next you will find a section on salads and dressings to serve with a good salad. There are many sauces in which olive oil is an essential ingredient, for it has the ability to blend with different flavours and many kinds of food. Perhaps the most famous of all sauces using olive oil is the *true* mayonnaise. Did you know that mayonnaise was first created in Spain? To make mayonnaise is not difficult when you have mastered the 'knack' and indeed in these days with modern electric mixers and liquidisers (blenders) a home-made mayonnaise is really very quick *and* simple to prepare. When you have made the basic mayonnaise recipe try some of the interesting variations given in this book.

I have given a selection of some of my favourite savoury dishes ranging from soups to fish, egg and meat recipes. I hope you enjoy cooking and eating these as much as I do in my own home. You will find in each dish that olive oil plays a very essential part. Sometimes, as in a soup such as Gazpacho, the olive oil is the secret of the smooth rich texture; in the fish and meat dishes the oil adds flavour and keeps the food moist.

I wonder if you have made pastry or cakes with olive oil? I have carried out many experiments using oil in baking and the results are extremely good. Quite often people are advised to use oil in baking for medical reasons and I think they have been pleasantly surprised at their success. Short crust pastry made with oil is crisp and light in texture; cakes, whether a light sponge or richer cake, are quickly prepared and keep moist and fresh for quite a long time.

When planning our menus I think most of us consider first of all the kind of dishes we know our family enjoys; and then plan the whole meal or day's meals from the point of view of a well balanced diet. We appreciate the importance of an adequate amount of protein to ensure healthy growth in children and to maintain health in adults and the necessity of having an adequate amount of fat and carbohydrates to promote a feeling of warmth, well-being and energy. At the same time most of us try to 'cut-down' on unnecessary carbohydrates and calories. You will find all the recipes in this section give you a clear indication of the essential food value plus calories in every dish.

I believe that money spent on good, pure and wholesome foods is money wisely invested.

A well planned diet, which includes plenty of fresh foods, plays a very essential part in keeping us all fit and energetic. Happy meal times, with interesting dishes, are a valuable contribution to enjoyable family living. I am sure you will agree with me that Spanish olive oil, one of the natural foods of today, can help produce delicious home cooking.

Marguerite Patten

Marguerite Patten has been called England's Cookery Queen.
Well known as writer, demonstrator, home economist, radio and TV cookery expert, Mrs Patten in a distinguished culinary career has completely justified the Daily Mail's description of her as "one of this country's most famous and popular cooks".
After wartime service as a senior demonstrator with the Ministry of Food, Mrs Patten ran Harrods Food and Home Service Advice Bureau for seven years.
She was one of the earliest contributors to BBC's Woman's Hour and became the regular cookery expert on the first TV women's magazine programme **Designed for Women** in 1947. When the BBC started their Cookery Club in 1956 she was appointed President and was associated with the programme for five years. She still broadcasts regularly in Woman's Hour and in 1973 started a new TV cookery series. As well as on television, Mrs Patten has given public demonstrations in numerous British towns and cities—even at the London Palladium—as well as in Australia.
She has contributed cookery columns to many newspapers and magazines and is regular cookery contributor to the national magazine Woman's Own. She has written 75 books and cookery card sets for adults as well as school use and world sales of her publications now top ten millions. Her book Cookery in Colour, published by Paul Hamlyn in 1960, has broken all cookbook records with a sale total of 1½ million copies.

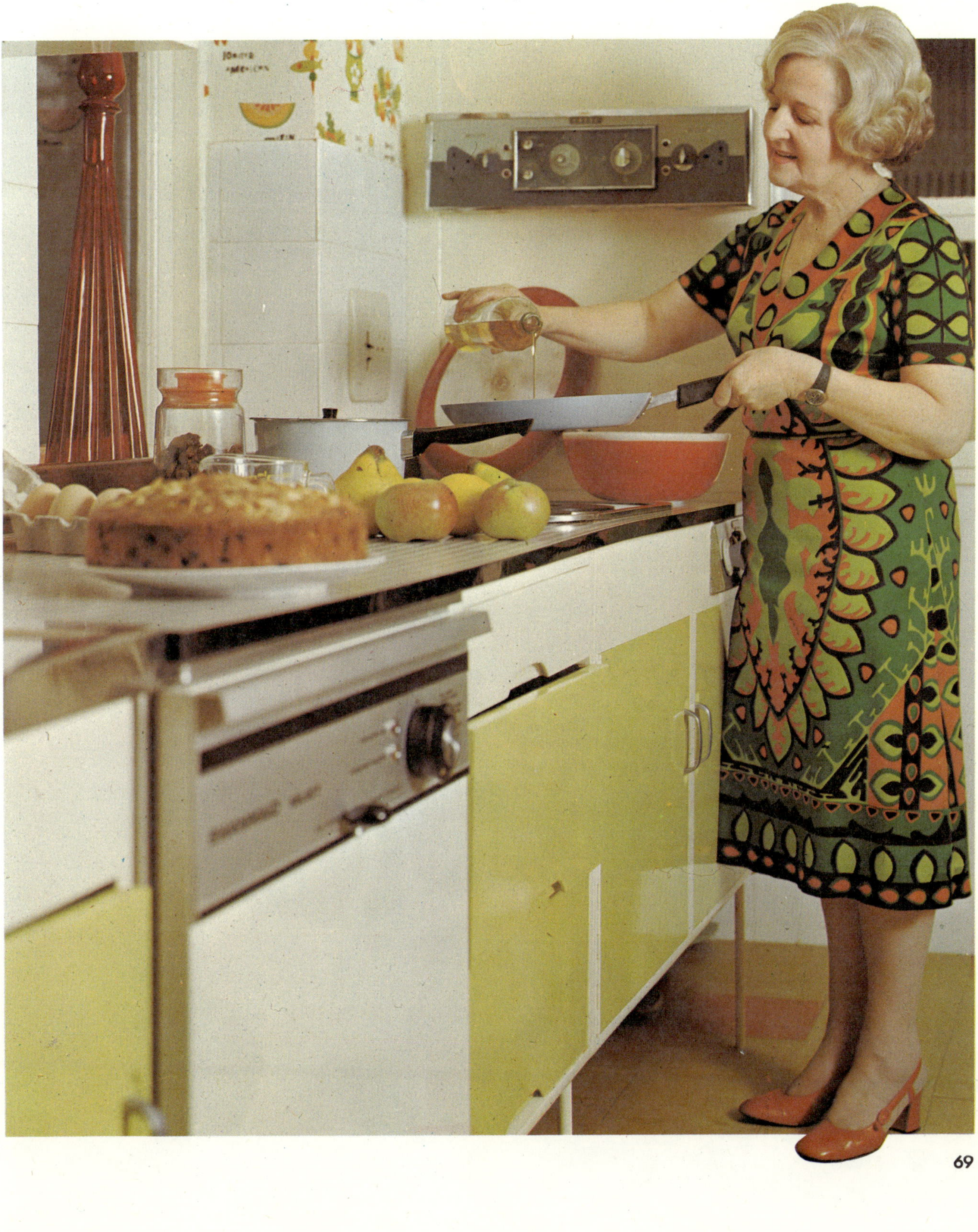

STARTERS

The first course of a meal is a very important one; it should be interesting but not too filling; indeed it should sharpen one's appetite for the main course ahead. Here are some of my favourite recipes to serve as a first course.

VICHYSSOISE

4 medium leeks
2 tablespoons Spanish olive oil
1¼ pints chicken stock
2 medium potatoes
1 tablespoon chopped parsley
1 tablespoon chopped chives
seasoning
¼ pint thin or thick cream
to garnish: 1 tablespoon chopped
chives

Prepare the leeks, chop, then toss in hot oil until pale golden, but do not brown. Add stock, peeled chopped potatoes, parsley and chives. Season well and simmer gently for 30 minutes. Rub through a fine sieve; when cool gradually add cream. Season to taste when quite cold. Serve very cold, garnished with chopped chives.

SERVES 4 (generous helping)

Each portion contains
270 Calories/19g carbohydrate
20g fat/4g protein
(Using single cream)

CHEESE AND CARROT SOUP

1 large onion
3 large carrots
2 tablespoons Spanish olive oil
1 oz flour
½ pint chicken stock or water and
½ chicken stock cube
seasoning
4 — 6 oz grated Cheddar cheese
to garnish: 1 — 2 tablespoons
grated raw carrot
1 — 2 tablespoons chopped chives

Peel and grate the onion and carrots. Toss the vegetables in the hot oil for several minutes; do not over-cook. Stir in the flour then blend in the liquid. Bring to the boil and cook until thickened. Season lightly. Stir in the grated cheese *just before serving,* heat for 1 — 2 minutes only, taste, add more seasoning and top with the carrot and chives.

SERVES 4

Each portion contains
310 Calories/11g carbohydrate
26g fat/11g protein

AVOCADO VINAIGRETTE

for the dressing:
¼ teaspoon French mustard
pinch sugar
shake pepper
pinch salt
3 tablespoons Spanish olive oil
1½ — 2 tablespoons lemon juice
2 firm ripe avocado pears
to garnish: lemon, tomato

Make the dressing first, for avocado pears discolour easily if halved and left to stand (unless they are generously sprinkled with lemon juice). Blend the mustard, sugar, pepper and salt, then work in the oil and then the lemon juice. Normally a vinaigrette dressing has twice as much oil as lemon juice (or use malt or wine vinegar), but I like a rather sharp dressing for avocado pears. Halve the pears, remove the stones. Put on to the serving plates and garnish with wedges of lemon and/or tomato. Spoon as much dressing as desired into the centre of the pears and serve. Any dressing left can be stored in a screw topped jar, in fact it is worth while making a large quantity and storing this, so you always have a good vinaigrette dressing available.

SERVES 4

Each portion contains
235 Calories/trace carbohydrate
24g fat/trace protein

To vary the dressing
Add finely chopped fresh herbs.
Add 1 — 2 crushed cloves garlic or a little garlic salt.

ARTICHOKES WITH LEMON MAYONNAISE

4 globe artichokes
seasoning
2 teaspoons Spanish olive oil
1 lemon
4 — 6 tablespoons mayonnaise (qv)
to garnish: parsley

Cut the stalks from the artichokes and the top of the leaves. Put into boiling and well seasoned water with the olive oil (this gives the artichokes a pleasant shine and improves the flavour). Cook until the base of the leaves and the artichoke hearts are tender (this takes 20 — 25 minutes, according to size). Drain the artichokes and cool slightly, then remove centres of the vegetables. Grate the lemon rind finely, squeeze out the juice and blend with the mayonnaise. Spoon the mayonnaise into the centres of the artichokes and top with parsley.

SERVES 4

Each portion contains
275 Calories/trace carbohydrate
29g fat/12g protein

PIZZA ALLA NAPOLETANA

for the dough:
¼oz fresh yeast or 1 teaspoon dried yeast
4 tablespoons warm water
8 oz plain flour
good pinch salt
1 tablespoon Spanish olive oil
for the topping:
1 onion
1 clove garlic (optional)
2 tablespoons Spanish olive oil
1 lb tomatoes
seasoning
½ teaspoon chopped fresh oregano or pinch dried oregano
3 — 4 oz Gruyère or Mozzarella cheese
few canned anchovy fillets
8 — 9 black olives
to garnish: parsley or watercress

Cream fresh yeast and add the warm water. If using dried yeast sprinkle on the water. Leave for 10 minutes in a warm place. Sieve flour and salt, add olive oil then yeast liquid. Knead until a smooth dough, put into a bowl and cover with polythene or a cloth, leave for 1 — 1¼ hours or until the dough doubles its size.
Meanwhile chop or grate the peeled onion and garlic. Heat 1½ tablespoons olive oil and toss the onion and garlic in this for 3 — 4 minutes, add the skinned chopped tomatoes, simmer for 10 minutes in an open pan until a thick purée, add seasoning and herbs. Knead yeast dough and roll into 7 — 8 inch round. Brush with remaining olive oil, put on a warmed baking tray; top with tomato mixture. Leave to rise for 20 minutes. Bake for 10 minutes in centre of a hot oven. Top with thinly sliced cheese, anchovy fillets and halved olives, bake for another 10 minutes. Serve hot or cold garnished with parsley or watercress.

SERVES 4

Each portion contains
570 Calories/49g carbohydrate
30g fat/16g protein

STUFFED MUSHROOMS

8 – 12 large mushrooms
1 large onion
3 tablespoons Spanish olive oil
2 oz cooked long grain rice
6 oz minced cooked meat
1 fresh bay leaf or small portion dried bay leaf
2 – 3 rosemary leaves or pinch dried rosemary
2 – 3 sage leaves or pinch dried sage
seasoning
1 tablespoon tomato purée
to garnish: chopped parsley

Remove the stalks from the mushrooms. Wash the caps well, but do not peel. Chop the mushroom stalks and onion very finely. Heat 2 tablespoons of the oil in a frying pan and fry the mushroom caps for 2 – 3 minutes only. Lift out of the oil and put into an oven-proof dish, together with the remaining 1 tablespoon oil.
Toss the chopped mushroom stalks and onion in the oil remaining in the frying pan for a few minutes, then blend with the rice, meat, finely chopped herbs or dried herbs, seasoning and tomato purée. Pile this mixture into the mushroom caps. Cover the dish with foil or a lid and bake for 15 minutes towards the top of a moderately hot oven, 375 – 400°F (190 – 200°C),
Gas Mark 5 – 6. Garnish with chopped parsley. Serve as a light main dish or hors d'oeuvre.

SERVES 4

Each portion contains
330 Calories/6g carbohydrate
28g fat/14g protein

SEAFOOD COCKTAIL CAPRICE

for the sauce:
5 tablespoons mayonnaise (qv)
1 tablespoon tomato purée
2 tablespoons thick cream
1 tablespoon white vinegar or lemon juice or sherry
seasoning
for the fish mixture:
2 dessert apples
1 — 2 tablespoons lemon juice
2 sticks celery
¼ cucumber
6 — 8 oz shell fish (use all shelled
prawns or all crabmeat or a mixture of fish)
to garnish: black olives, parsley

Blend all the ingredients for the sauce together. Core the apples, but do not peel. Slice about half of one apple thinly and dice the remainder. Sprinkle with lemon juice to keep a good colour. Chop the celery finely, cut a few slices of cucumber, but dice the remainder.
Mix the diced apple, celery and diced cucumber with the fish and dressing. Put into 4 — 6 individual dishes or 1 large one as shown. Garnish with olives, parsley, sliced cucumber and sliced apple.

SERVES 4 — 6

Each portion contains
255 Calories/7g carbohydrate
22g fat/7g protein
(Based on the dish serving 6)

Variations
Serve on a bed of shredded lettuce. Omit the apples, celery, cucumber and serve the fish in the sauce.

MAYONNAISE

2 egg yolks
good shake pepper
½ teaspoon salt
½ — 1 teaspoon dry mustard
½ — 1 teaspoon sugar
8 — 12 tablespoons Spanish olive oil
1 — 2 tablespoons lemon juice or vinegar
1 — 2 tablespoons boiling water (optional)

To make in a bowl Make sure egg yolks are at room temperature. Put yolks into a dry bowl, beat in seasonings and sugar (use a wooden spoon, a hand or electric whisk on low speed). Gradually beat in the olive oil; start by adding this drop by drop then 'speed up' slightly as the sauce thickens. (The amount of oil used is purely a matter of personal taste, the more oil the richer the mayonnaise and the thicker it becomes.)
When mayonnaise has thickened add the lemon juice or vinegar. Lastly beat in the boiling water; this is not essential but it gives a particularly light 'fluffy' texture to the sauce, taste and adjust seasonings.
In a liquidiser (blender) This enables you to make the mayonnaise in 1 or 2 minutes. Remove the cap from the lid or prepare to tilt the lid slightly to prevent splashing, or put a layer of foil over the top of the goblet and make a hole in this through which to pour the oil. Use the same ingredients as above but due to the efficiency of blending you can use whole eggs if you prefer, so use 2 whole eggs or 1 large egg or 1 whole egg and 1 yolk — the more white you use the lighter the mayonnaise. Put the eggs or yolks into the *dry* liquidiser goblet, add the seasonings, sugar, lemon juice or vinegar. Switch to medium speed until blended. Pour the olive oil in a steady stream through the 'hole' in the lid with the motor running at medium speed, then add boiling water at the end.

SERVES 6 (generous helping)

Each portion contains
470 Calories/3g carbohydrate
51g fat/trace protein

Variations

Fennel Mayonnaise (delicious with fish) Add little chopped white stem and green leaves of fennel.
Green Mayonnaise Add chopped parsley and other herbs.
Lemon Mayonnaise Add the finely grated rind of a lemon plus little extra lemon juice.
Tartare Sauce Add ½ — 1 tablespoon chopped gherkins, ½ — 1 tablespoon chopped capers and ½ — 1 tablespoon chopped parsley.
Tomato Mayonnaise Sieve 2 large ripe tomatoes and blend with the mayonnaise, or use tomato ketchup to taste. If to serve over fish salads, give more flavour by adding a few drops either Worcestershire, chilli. Tabasco, or soy sauce.

Use various kinds of vinegar (tarragon, chilli, etc.); flavour mayonnaise with horseradish, curry powder, etc.

FISH DISHES

We are fortunate in having a wide variety of fish in this country so fish dishes should never be dull.
Time the cooking carefully when you cook fish, for over-cooking spoils both flavour and appearance.

PERFECT FRIED FISH

The success of fried fish is in the way it is fried and the kind of coating used.

The oil must be really hot before the fish is fried; details of shallow and deep frying are given below. The coating gives a pleasant colour and crispness to the outside of the fish and keeps the flesh moist inside. You have a choice of three kinds of coating:
a) Seasoned flour (or seasoned oatmeal — particularly good with herrings). This coating is not good for deep frying.
b) A light coating of seasoned flour then beaten egg and crumbs. Most people use crisp breadcrumbs but fine soft crumbs could be used. This coating is equally good for shallow or deep frying.
c) A light coating of seasoned flour then a batter (see recipe for apple fritters). This coating can be used for shallow or deep frying, but is better for the latter.

To coat the fish
Wash and dry the fish. Put the seasoned flour on a plate or dish or sheet of greaseproof paper or into a polythene or greaseproof bag. Dip the fish in this and press firmly, or shake vigorously into the flour. Make sure the fish is evenly coated. Shake off the surplus flour before continuing with another coating or frying.

Brush the beaten egg over the fish, then coat in crumbs, using the method, above, given for flour.
Pat the crumbs firmly into the fish with a palette knife so there are no loose crumbs.

Put the batter into a large container, dip the fish in this, hold over the container just before frying so the surplus batter runs off the fish.

To fry fish

Fish may be fried in shallow or deep Spanish olive oil.

Shallow frying Coat fish as above. Heat 2 — 3 tablespoons olive oil (if frying thin fillets) or 3 — 4 tablespoons olive oil (if frying thicker pieces of fish) in a large frying pan. Test the temperature of the oil (see under deep frying), put in coated fish and cook for:
4 minutes — thin fillets of fish (turn after 2 minutes and cook for the same time on the second side);
5 — 6 minutes — thicker fillets (cook as above, lower heat for final 1 — 2 minutes);
7 — 9 minutes — thick pieces or whole fish (cook as thin fillets, then lower heat for the final 3 — 5 minutes).
Drain on absorbent paper (see under deep frying).
Deep frying Coat fish as above. Heat the olive oil in a deep frying container or saucepan with the frying basket in position. This makes sure the fish will not stick to the basket. NEVER have the pan more than half full of oil. Test to see if oil is the right temperature: a cooking thermometer should read 365°F. (185°C.), but a cube of day-old bread should turn golden brown in *under* 1 minute. Lower fish carefully into frying basket, then reduce heat slightly so the fish cooks steadily. Cook for:
3 minutes — thin fillets of fish;
4 minutes — thicker fillets of fish;
5 minutes — thick pieces or steaks of fish.
Lift fish in frying basket out of pan, hold basket over the pan for a few seconds so that surplus oil drains back into it.
Tip fish on to crumpled tissue or kitchen paper on a hot plate or tin; this drains excess oil and makes sure the fish is really crisp.

Fried fish is generally garnished with lemon and parsley or as picture with watercress, lemon and tomato, and served with tartare sauce (qv).

PERFECT FRIED POTATOES

Peel and slice the potatoes or cut into chips; dry well in a cloth or absorbent paper before frying.

Shallow frying Put enough Spanish olive oil into the pan to give a depth of ½ to ¾ inch. Heat oil (test as instructions given under deep frying of fish). Fry steadily until golden brown on one side, then turn and fry on the second side until golden brown and tender. You could remove and fry twice, as under deep frying, but this is not essential. Drain well on absorbent paper.

Deep frying Heat the oil and frying basket (test as instructions given under deep frying of fish). DO NOT OVER-FILL PAN. Put in some prepared potatoes. Fry steadily in the hot oil until the potatoes are soft, but still light in colour. Lift out of the oil, reheat this, then fry the potatoes for the second time until crisp and golden brown, this will take only 2 minutes, approximately. Drain well on absorbent paper.
Note To re-use olive oil pour through a fine strainer or muslin into the bottle or container.

CURRIED FISH SCALLOPS

1 onion
1 apple
1 tablespoon Spanish olive oil
2 teaspoons curry powder
2 teaspoons cornflour
½ pint water
seasoning
squeeze lemon juice
12 oz cod or other white fish
2 oz shelled prawns
1 lb cooked potatoes
1 oz margarine
little milk
to garnish: tomatoes, parsley

Peel and grate the onion and apple. Heat the olive oil and toss the onion, apple and curry powder in this for several minutes. Stir in the cornflour, then add the water, seasoning and lemon juice. Bring the sauce to the boil and cook for 10 minutes. Put the diced white fish into the sauce and simmer for 10 minutes, then add the prawns and heat for a few minutes. Mash the potatoes with the margarine and milk. Pipe into 8 scallop shells (see picture) and brown for a few minutes under a hot grill. Spoon the fish mixture into the shells and garnish with pieces of tomato and parsley.

SERVES 4 as a main course, 8 as an hors d'oeuvre

Each portion contains
170 Calories/19g carbohydrate
7g fat/10g protein
(Based on the dish serving 8)

STUFFED CODLING

1 codling about 2½ — 3 lb
for the filling:
3 tablespoons Spanish olive oil
1 — 2 slices bread
1 — 2 oz blanched almonds
1 — 2 oz currants or other dried fruit
seasoning
1 lemon
to garnish: 1 lemon, watercress, radishes

Split the codling and remove the backbone, but leave the head on the fish. To prepare the filling heat 2 tablespoons of the olive oil then cut the bread into small dice, removing the crusts. Fry in the oil until golden, mix with the almonds, dried fruit, seasoning and grated lemon rind and juice. Put into the fish and lift into a well oiled baking dish. Brush top of fish with remaining oil and bake for 35 minutes in centre of moderate oven, 350 — 375°F (180 — 190°C), Gas Mark 4 — 5. Garnish with lemon, watercress and radishes.

SERVES 4
Each portion contains
560 Calories/20g carbohydrate
31g fat/52g protein

POACHED SKATE WITH HERBED RICE

¼ pint white wine
½ pint water
seasoning
bunch fresh herbs
1 tablespoon Spanish olive oil
4 portions skate
for the rice mixture:
¾ pint fish stock, see method
1 tablespoon chopped parsley
¼ teaspoon chopped lemon thyme or pinch dried thyme
1 clove garlic
6 oz long grain rice
for the topping:
1 tablespoon Spanish olive oil
4 thin slices processed or Gruyère cheese
1 tablespoon chopped parsley

Put the wine, water and seasoning into a large saucepan, together with the herbs (tied with cotton or in muslin) and the oil. Bring to simmering point then add the skate. Simmer the liquid until the skate is nearly tender (about 10 minutes), do not over-cook. Lift the fish on to a dish and put on one side. Strain the fish stock from the pan, if necessary add a little more wine or water to make up to ¾ pint. Return the stock to the pan. Add the herbs, crushed clove garlic and rice. Bring liquid to the boil, stir briskly, cover the pan and simmer for 15 minutes or until the rice is tender. Add more seasoning if required. When the rice is nearly cooked brush the skate with the oil and heat for 3 — 4 minutes under the grill.
Top with the cheese and heat for a further 1 — 2 minutes, until the cheese melts; do not allow it to brown.
Put the rice on to the serving dish, top with chopped parsley and the portions of fish.

SERVES 4
Each portion contains
610 Calories/34g carbohydrate
35g fat/42g protein
Variations
Use other fish instead of skate.
Keep the skate in one large piece and cut into portions after cooking; in which case increase cooking time in the wine liquid to about 20 minutes.

79

MEAT DISHES

The recipes in this section vary from the luxurious steaks or fillets of veal to the economical chuck steak.

SCALOPPINE ALLA BOLOGNESE

4 thin slices (fillets) veal weighing about 6 oz each
seasoning
1 thick slice fat bacon — about 6 oz
3 tablespoons Spanish olive oil
few tablespoons white wine
3 — 4 oz grated Gruyère or Mozzarella cheese
to garnish: parsley

Cut each fillet of veal into 2 — 3 pieces and season well. Cut the bacon into neat fingers. Heat the olive oil in a heavy flame-proof pan and fry the veal and bacon steadily for 10 — 12 minutes until tender; turn several times. Add just enough wine to moisten the meat. Top with the cheese and heat for a few minutes over the heat, or under the grill, until the cheese melts. Garnish with parsley.

SERVES 4

Each portion contains
170 Calories/trace carbohydrate
11g fat/17g protein

BARBECUED STEAK

Steak, cut in one piece, weighing 1½ lb — rump, sirloin or porterhouse
1 tablespoon tomato ketchup
1 teaspoon made mustard
2 tablespoons red wine
2 tablespoons Spanish olive oil
seasoning
for the rice mixture:
2 tablespoons Spanish olive oil
4 — 6 oz mushrooms
6 oz long grain rice
¾ pint water
for the onion rings:
1 large onion
1 egg
1 oz cornflour
3 tablespoons water
Spanish olive oil for frying
to garnish: parsley

Tie the steak into a neat shape if necessary. Mix the ketchup, mustard, wine and olive oil together, season well. Pour into dish. Stand the steak in this for about 30 minutes, turning once or twice. Meanwhile heat the oil for the rice mixture in a pan. Fry the thickly sliced mushrooms in the oil, add the rice, turn once or twice so the rice does not dry, add the water and seasoning and bring to the boil. Stir briskly. Cover the pan and simmer over the barbecue fire for 15 minutes. Peel and slice the onion; separate the slices into rings. Mix the egg yolk, cornflour and water then fold in seasoning and the stiffly whisked egg white. Dip the onion rings in this and fry in hot oil until crisp and brown. Cook the steak to personal taste over the hot barbecue; brush it with any oil and tomato ketchup mixture that remains and turn frequently. Serve with the rice mixture and onion rings and garnish with parsley.

SERVES 4

Each portion contains
815 Calories/23g carbohydrate
62g fat/42g protein

SPICY STEAK

for the marinade:
3 tablespoons Spanish olive oil
1 tablespoon brown vinegar or red wine
1 – 2 crushed cloves garlic
seasoning
½ teaspoon ground cinnamon or grated nutmeg

piece steak about 1¼ lb and about ½ – ¾ inch in thickness (choose thick rump, sirloin or porterhouse steak)
to garnish: small can anchovy fillets, few stuffed olives

Put the oil, vinegar or wine, garlic seasoning and cinnamon or nutmeg into a large shallow dish. Place the steak in this and leave for about 1 hour, turning several times. Lift the steak from the marinade, place on the grill pan. Put under a hot grill and cook for 10 – 15 minutes, depending upon personal taste. Turn the steak once or twice during cooking and brush with any remaining marinade or a little more Spanish olive oil. Remove the steak from under the grill, top with well drained anchovy fillets and sliced stuffed olives. Return to the grill for 1 minute only then serve. A green salad or broccoli is an excellent accompaniment to this dish.

SERVES 4

Each portion contains
550 Calories/trace carbohydrate
46g fat/33g protein

VEAL GOULASH

1½ lb lean veal
1 tablespoon flour
1 tablespoon paprika
seasoning
3 tablespoons Spanish olive oil
1 – 2 onions
1 lb tomatoes
¼ – ½ pint white stock or water and
½ chicken stock cube
to garnish: large sprig of parsley
to serve: boiled rice

Dice the veal. Mix the flour, paprika and seasoning. Coat the veal in this and toss in the hot olive oil. Peel and dice or slice the onions and tomatoes, add to the veal together with ¼ pint stock or water and stock cube. Simmer for about 1½ hours. Stir from time to time and add any extra liquid required, but this should be a thick mixture. Garnish with parsley. Serve with boiled rice.

SERVES 4 – 6

Each portion contains
355 Calories/7g carbohydrate
19g fat/41g protein
(Based on the dish serving 6)

BEEF WITH ORANGES

1½ lb chuck steak
2 oranges
2 onions
6 — 12 small carrots
seasoning
1 oz flour
2 tablespoons Spanish olive oil
1 pint brown stock or water and
1 — 2 beef stock cubes
to garnish: 1 small orange, parsley

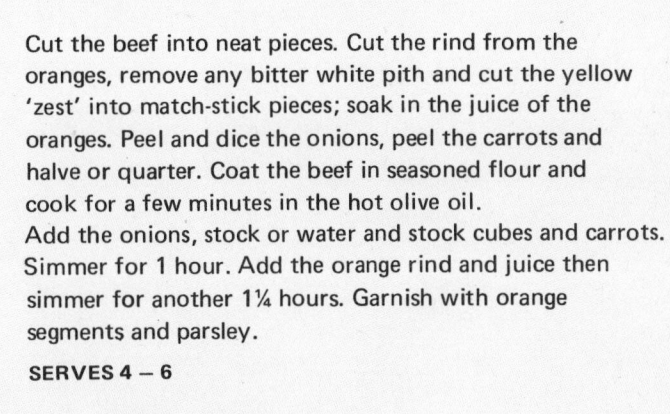

Cut the beef into neat pieces. Cut the rind from the oranges, remove any bitter white pith and cut the yellow 'zest' into match-stick pieces; soak in the juice of the oranges. Peel and dice the onions, peel the carrots and halve or quarter. Coat the beef in seasoned flour and cook for a few minutes in the hot olive oil.
Add the onions, stock or water and stock cubes and carrots. Simmer for 1 hour. Add the orange rind and juice then simmer for another 1¼ hours. Garnish with orange segments and parsley.

SERVES 4 — 6

Each portion contains
300 Calories/12g carbohydrate
16g fat/29g protein
(Based on the dish serving 6)

PORK AND CRANBERRY KEBABS

for the marinade:
4 tablespoons Spanish olive oil
seasoning
1 clove garlic (optional)
for the kebabs:
8 — 10 oz lean shoulder pork
4 lambs' kidneys
4 rashers streaky bacon
½ small cucumber
4 firm ripe tomatoes
8 small sausages
for the glaze:
1 — 2 tablespoons cranberry jelly
2 tablespoons water
to serve: 6 — 8 oz cooked long grain rice

Put the oil, seasoning and crushed garlic clove into a shallow dish. Cut the meat into 1 — inch cubes; skin, core and halve the kidneys. Put the meat into the seasoned oil and leave for 20 minutes, turning once or twice. Remove the rind from the bacon and roll neatly. Cut the cucumber into 8 slices and halve the tomatoes; season the vegetables lightly. Lift the meat from the marinade and put on to long metal skewers with the rest of the ingredients (see picture). Put the cranberry jelly, water and any of the oil mixture left into a saucepan and heat until the jelly melts. Brush the kebabs with this glaze and cook under a hot grill or over a barbecue fire for approximately 15 minutes. Turn frequently and baste with the jelly mixture. Serve on a bed of cooked rice.

SERVES 4

Each portion contains
510 Calories/34g carbohydrate
29g fat/30g protein

SCOTCH CUTLETS WITH MINT JELLY

4 cutlets lamb
2½ tablespoons mint jelly
seasoning
3 tablespoons Spanish olive oil
12 oz — 1 lb pork sausagemeat
1 egg
2 oz fine breadcrumbs
(preferably soft crumbs)
to garnish: parsley

Trim the cutlets if necessary. Melt the jelly until a spreading consistency; brush the meat on both sides with about half of this, season well. Heat 1 tablespoon of the oil in a large frying pan and cook the cutlets for 10 minutes, turning once or twice. Lift out of the pan and allow to cool. Coat the cooked cutlets with the remainder of the jelly then with the sausagemeat. Brush with beaten egg and coat in the crumbs. Heat the remainder of the oil in the pan and fry the cutlets for approximately 10 minutes, until the sausagemeat is cooked and the coating crisp and brown.
Drain on absorbent paper, put a cutlet frill on each cutlet then serve. Garnish with sprigs of parsley.
A crisp salad and jacket potatoes, topped with butter or cream cheese, are delicious with this dish.

SERVES 4
Each portion contains
845 Calories/30g carbohydrate
72g fat/22g protein

BEEF RISSOLES

1 onion or several spring onions
1 tablespoon Spanish olive oil
12 oz cooked minced beef
2 oz soft breadcrumbs
1 egg
seasoning
to coat: little flour
to fry: 2 tablespoons Spanish
    olive oil

Chop the onion or spring onions and fry in the 1 tablespoon hot olive oil. Add the beef, crumbs, egg and seasoning. Allow the mixture to cool and stiffen then form into 4 large or 8 smaller round cakes. Coat lightly with seasoned flour. Fry in hot oil until crisp and brown. Serve with salad or a green vegetable.

SERVES 4

Each portion contains
485 Calories 13g carbohydrate
38g fat/22g protein

Variations
Bind the meat and crumbs with a thick sauce made with 1 oz fat, 1 oz flour, ¼ pint stock instead of the egg. Coat the rissoles with flour then beaten egg and crumbs. Add a crushed clove garlic to the onion and chopped gherkins and capers to the meat mixture.
Use other meat or poultry.

CURRIED VEAL RISOTTO

1½ — 2 lb veal shoulder
½ — 1 tablespoon curry powder
2 tablespoons Spanish olive oil
6 oz long grain rice
1 large packet mixed frozen
vegetables or equivalent in
fresh vegetables
1 large onion
1½ pints chicken stock or water
and 2 chicken stock cubes
seasoning
to garnish: 1 — 2 canned red
peppers, parsley

Dice the meat and coat in the curry powder then toss in the hot olive oil for 8 — 10 minutes, until well browned. Put the rice, vegetables, chopped onion and stock or water and stock cubes into a saucepan, add the seasoning and cook for about 5 minutes. Stir well then transfer to a deep casserole (allow space for rice to swell).
Put the veal on top of the rice mixture.
Cover the casserole and bake for 1 hour in the centre of a very moderate to moderate oven, 325 — 350°F (170 — 180°C), Gas Mark 3 — 4. Remove the lid and garnish with the peppers and parsley.

SERVES 4 — 6

Each portion contains
330 Calories/13g carbohydrate
14g fat/37g protein
(Based on the dish serving 6)

87

SWEET AND SOUR MEAT BALLS

for the meat balls:
1 onion
2 tablespoons Spanish olive oil
1 dessert apple
1 lb minced beef
1 oz flour
seasoning
1 egg
1 tablespoon milk or stock
1 — 2 teaspoons chopped parsley

for the sauce, etc.:
2 tablespoons Spanish olive oil
1 medium can pineapple rings
1 level tablespoon cornflour
1 tablespoon brown malt vinegar
½ tablespoon soy sauce
1 oz sugar
2 tablespoons mustard pickle
1 dessert apple
small piece green pepper
small piece red pepper

Peel and chop or grate the onion and toss in the hot olive oil for 5 minutes. Add the peeled diced apple and minced beef and cook for another 5 minutes.
Stir the mixture well so it does not become hard.
Add the rest of the ingredients for the meat balls.
Form into 8 — 12 balls.
Note This is a basic meat ball recipe that can be varied by adding various flavourings. The meat balls shown with the spaghetti Milanaise (qv) are as above, but *without* the apple. Add 2 tablespoons milk or stock.
To cook the meat balls: Heat the olive oil in a large frying pan. Turn the meat balls in the oil for 10 minutes then lift on to a plate. Drain the syrup from the pineapple rings and if necessary add water to make up to ½ pint. Blend with the cornflour and pour into the pan. Stir over a low heat until thickened, then add the vinegar, soy sauce and sugar. Replace the meat balls in this sauce and simmer for 15 minutes, then add the diced pickle, cored and thinly sliced apple, diced pineapple and strips of red and green peppers.
Heat for a few minutes only.

SERVES 4 — 6
Each portion contains
360 Calories/16g carbohydrate
23g fat/24g protein
(Based on the dish serving 6)

SAVOURY MEAT RING

2 large onions
3 — 4 large tomatoes
3 tablespoons Spanish olive oil
1½ lb minced raw beef
3 oz soft white breadcrumbs
1 tablespoon chopped parsley
2 eggs
¼ pint milk or brown stock
pinch dried marjoram or oregano
seasoning
to garnish: watercress, little chopped parsley, cooked peas and onions

Peel and chop the onions and tomatoes fairly coarsely. Heat nearly all the oil in a large pan and toss the onions and tomatoes in this for 3 — 4 minutes only. Meanwhile coat a 9 — 10 inch ring mould and piece of foil with the remaining oil. Mix the rest of the ingredients (except the garnish) with the onions and tomatoes, press into the prepared mould, cover with the foil. Stand in a container of cold water (to prevent drying) and cook for 1¾ hours in centre of very moderate oven, 325°F (170°C), Gas Mark 3. Invert over hot serving dish, press watercress leaves and parsley into ring; fill centre with peas and onions.

SERVES UP TO 8
Each portion contains
285 Calories/7g carbohydrate
17g fat/28g protein
(Based on the dish serving 8)

POULTRY AND GAME

Chicken has become one of the most economical foods. It is also extremely versatile as it can be cooked in a great variety of ways.

The traditional jugged hare is one of the most delicious game dishes. You can use the same recipe for cooking rabbit or game birds.

FRIED CHICKEN AND HERBS

4 portions frying chicken
1 oz flour
seasoning
1 — 2 teaspoons chopped parsley
¼ teaspoon chopped rosemary
¼ teaspoon chopped lemon thyme
2 onions
4 — 5 cooked potatoes
4 tablespoons Spanish olive oil
to garnish: small piece green pepper, parsley

Wash and dry the chicken portions. Mix the flour, seasoning and herbs. Coat the chicken with the herb mixture. Peel and dice the onions and dice the potatoes. Heat half the oil in a large frying pan and fry the onion until tender. Lift on to a dish and keep hot. Add the remainder of the oil and fry the chicken portions for 15 minutes, until golden brown and tender. Add the diced potato towards the end of the cooking time and brown this. Garnish with narrow strips of pepper and parsley.

SERVES 4

Each portion contains
605 Calories/16g carbohydrate
37g fat/35g protein

Variation
Use finely diced and par-boiled celery in place of onions. Toss the celery in the oil for a few minutes.

LEMON CHICKEN

for the rice mixture:
¾ pint water
pinch saffron powder
juice 1 lemon
2 tablespoons Spanish olive oil
2 – 3 small potatoes
few sticks celery
6 oz long grain rice
½ – 1 green pepper
½ – 1 red pepper
seasoning

4 chicken joints
finely grated rind 1 lemon
2 tablespoons flour
3 tablespoons Spanish olive oil
to garnish: watercress, chopped parsley

Mix the water, saffron powder and lemon juice.
Heat the olive oil for the rice mixture and toss the peeled diced raw potatoes, chopped celery and rice in this.
Add the water, etc., bring liquid to the boil, lower the heat and cover the pan. Simmer for 10 minutes then add the diced peppers (discard cores and seeds) together with seasoning. Simmer for another 5 minutes. Meanwhile wash and dry the chicken; allow frozen chicken joints to thaw out. Mix the lemon rind, flour and seasoning and coat the chicken with this. Fry in the hot oil until tender and golden (about 15 minutes). Put the rice mixture in a dish and top with chicken and garnish.

SERVES 4

Each portion contains
680 Calories/14g carbohydrate
44g fat/40g protein

Variation
Fry the chicken joints for 5 minutes only in a large pan, remove then fry the potatoes, celery and rice.
Add the liquid, etc., return the chicken to the pan and cook altogether rather like a Paella.

JUGGED HARE

2 — 3 oz hare liver
seasoning
1 medium hare (ask the poulterer to save the blood of the hare)
1 tablespoon vinegar
2½ tablespoons Spanish olive oil
2 — 3 large onions
2 — 3 large carrots
2 oz flour
2 pints brown stock
1 bay leaf
bouquet garni
4 tablespoons port wine
2 tablespoons redcurrant jelly
to garnish: fried croûtons (see below)
to serve: redcurrant jelly

Put the liver into a small pan, add seasoning to taste and just enough water to cover; simmer for about 30 — 40 minutes. Meanwhile, soak jointed hare in cold water to which is added the vinegar, for about 1 hour; this whitens the flesh. Heat the oil and fry the sliced onions and carrots in this, then stir in the flour and cook for several minutes. Gradually add the brown stock and the blood of the hare. Bring the sauce to the boil, add the drained and dried hare and the herbs. Simmer for 1½ — 2 hours. Lift the game out of the sauce on to a plate, sieve the sauce and the well drained liver (this makes a great deal of difference to the flavour of the sauce). Return the sauce to the pan with the port wine and jelly; simmer for a few minutes, then return the game to the sauce and continue cooking until quite tender. While the game cooks, prepare and cook the fried croûtons (see below). Dish the hare on to a large plate and top with the fried croûtons. Serve with redcurrant jelly.

SERVES 6 (generous helping)

Each portion contains
365 Calories/8g carbohydrate
16g fat/32g protein
(excluding croûtons)

FRIED CROUTONS

Cut triangles, rounds or the traditional heart shapes from slices of bread. Fry in hot oil until crisp and golden brown. Drain on absorbent paper.

PASTA, RICE AND EGG DISHES

It is important that pasta is not over-cooked and sufficient water is used in cooking. Pasta makes an economical basis for a great variety of delicious dishes. Rice is a wonderful accompaniment to meat, fish, etc., as well as being the basis for classic dishes. Egg dishes are quick and simple to prepare and delicious to eat at almost any meal.

SPAGHETTI BOLOGNESE
(with meat sauce)

for the sauce:
3 tablespoons Spanish olive oil
½ — 1 clove garlic (optional)
1 onion
4 oz mushrooms
1 carrot
approximately 6 oz minced beef
1 can tomatoes or 1 tube or small can tomato purée
or 4 fresh tomatoes
seasoning
½ pint good brown stock if using tinned tomatoes
or ⅝ pint if using fresh tomatoes or purée
1 wineglass red wine

6 — 8 oz spaghetti
3 — 4 pints water
salt
to serve: grated Parmesan cheese
to garnish: parsley

Heat the oil in a pan, then gently fry the crushed garlic, finely chopped onion, mushrooms (keep whole if very small, chop if large) and shredded carrot for several minutes. Add the meat and the rest of the sauce ingredients and simmer for about 45 minutes, until the sauce has thickened. Meanwhile cook the spaghetti in boiling salted water until tender; strain. Pour the sauce on top of the cooked spaghetti and serve with the grated cheese. Garnish with parsley.

SERVES 4

Each portion contains
540 Calories/52g carbohydrate
30g fat/19g protein
(including Parmesan)

PEPPERED EGGS

2 large sized green peppers
seasoning
6 — 8 oz mushrooms
1 tablespoon Spanish olive oil
4 eggs
1 — 2 oz grated Cheddar cheese

Halve the peppers lengthways, remove the cores and seeds. Cook in well seasoned boiling water for 5 — 6 minutes only. Strain the peppers and put into an oven-proof dish. Wash and slice the mushrooms and cook in the hot oil for 2 — 3 minutes only; spoon into the pepper cases. Break the eggs on top of the sliced mushrooms, season and coat with the cheese.
Bake for **15 minutes** above the centre of a moderate oven 375°F (190°C), Gas Mark 5.

SERVES 4

Each portion contains
210 Calories/3g carbohydrate
17g fat/12g protein

SAVOURY EGGS

4 oz mushrooms
2 large onions
3 tablespoons Spanish olive oil
8 – 12 oz cooked potatoes
1 oz butter or margarine
2 – 3 tablespoons milk
5 eggs
3 – 4 oz grated cheese
seasoning
to garnish: chopped parsley

Wash and slice the mushrooms. Peel and chop the onions. Heat 2 tablespoons of the olive oil in a frying pan, fry the onions for 5 minutes, add the mushrooms, continue cooking for a further 5 minutes, lift out of the pan. Meanwhile mash the potatoes, add the butter or margarine, milk, 1 egg and the cheese; season well. Heat nearly all the remaining oil in the frying pan (save last of oil for poaching eggs – see note below). Put in the potato mixture, heat thoroughly, top with the onions and mushrooms. Finally poach the eggs, put on to the top of the potato mixture, garnish with parsley and serve at once.

SERVES 4

Each portion contains
525 Calories/23g carbohydrate
41g fat/18g protein

Note The eggs may be poached in boiling water or in well oiled cups over boiling water in an egg poacher (as in the picture). The latter gives a neater appearance.

SPANISH OMELETTE

1 large onion
4 oz cooked potatoes
1½ tablespoons Spanish olive oil
3 eggs
1 tablespoon water
seasoning

Peel and chop the onion and dice the potatoes. Heat 1 tablespoon of the oil in an omelette pan and cook the onion until tender then add the diced potatoes and heat through. Beat the eggs, water and seasoning then add the cooked onion and potatoes. Heat the rest of the oil in the pan, pour in the egg mixture and cook until just set. Slide on to a hot dish.

SERVES 1 – 2

Each portion contains
365 Calories/16g carbohydrate
29g fat/11g protein
(Based on the dish serving 2)

Variations
Use mixed diced vegetables instead of onion and potato.
Use diced cooked ham or shell fish with the vegetables.

SPAGHETTI MILANAISE
(with tomato sauce)

for the sauce:
1 clove garlic
1 onion
1 small dessert apple
2 tablespoons Spanish olive oil
1 small can tomatoes or 3 fresh tomatoes plus
3 tablespoons water
2 tablespoons tomato purée
¼ pint water
2 teaspoons cornflour
seasoning
1 teaspoon brown sugar

6 — 8 oz spaghetti
3 — 4 pints water
salt
1 tablespoon Spanish olive oil
to garnish: chopped parsley

Crush the clove garlic; peel and chop or grate the onion and apple. Heat the olive oil in a pan and toss the garlic, onion and apple in this for several minutes; take care the mixture does not become dark in colour.
Add the canned tomatoes and liquid from the can or the skinned fresh tomatoes and the 3 tablespoons water. Cover the pan and simmer gently for 10 minutes. Sieve the mixture if wished, or beat until fairly smooth. Return to the pan. Add the tomato purée and the water blended with the cornflour. Stir as the sauce comes to the boil and simmer until thickened and clear. Season the mixture well and add the sugar. Meanwhile cook the spaghetti in the boiling salted water until just tender; strain.
To give a particularly good texture to the pasta tip back into the pan with the oil, heat for 1 — 2 minutes.
Turn on to a dish and top with the tomato sauce; garnish with parsley. Serve with salad and grated cheese.

SERVES 4

Each portion contains
410 Calories/56g carbohydrate
20g fat/6g protein

Variation

Spaghetti Milanaise with Meat Balls Prepare the mixture as recipe for Sweet and Sour Meat Balls (qv). Form into small balls. Heat 2 tablespoons Spanish olive oil in a pan. Fry the meat balls rapidly for 2 — 3 minutes; turn once or twice. Add ¼ pint seasoned brown stock and simmer the meat balls for 10 minutes.
Drain and arrange on the hot spaghetti.

PAELLA

2 portions chicken or ½ small chicken
2 onions
1 carrot
1½ pints water
seasoning
good pinch saffron powder
3 tablespoons Spanish olive oil
1 — 2 cloves garlic
8 oz long grain rice
1 — 2 large tomatoes
about 1 pint mussels
small lobster
few large prawns
few slices choriza (spiced sausage)
to garnish: parsley or sage

Put the chicken, 1 peeled onion and carrot into a saucepan with 1 pint of the water and seasoning. Simmer for about 10 — 15 minutes only — the chicken should be very firm. Strain off the liquid, cut the chicken into smaller pieces; the onion and carrot can be discarded or chopped and added to the rice mixture towards the end of the cooking period. Measure the liquid and add enough water to give 1 pint again. Dissolve the saffron powder in the chicken liquid. Heat the olive oil in a large pan and fry the half cooked chicken and the second peeled and chopped onion and cloves garlic for 5 minutes. Add the rice and toss together, then blend in the saffron flavoured stock and quartered tomatoes; stir well, then simmer gently without covering pan. Meanwhile scrub the mussels, put into a saucepan with the remaining water and seasoning. *Discard any mussels that do not close when sharply tapped.* Heat for 6 — 8 minutes until mussels open — *discard any that do not open.* Continue to heat the rice until nearly tender; as the mixture dries out slightly add enough mussel liquid to keep it moist. When the rice is nearly tender add the pieces of lobster, prawns, mussels and choriza; heat for a few minutes. Garnish and serve.

SERVES 4 — 6 as a main dish

Each portion contains
340 Calories/14g carbohydrate
21g fat/24g protein
(Based on the dish serving 6)

Note This dish can be made more economically by adding shrimps or canned clams or cockles instead of prawns and lobster.
It is often usual to keep prawns, etc. in their shells (see picture) but easier to serve if the shells are removed first.

SALADS AND VEGETABLES

A good salad depends upon really fresh ingredients, prepared in an attractive fashion, *plus* a really good dressing in which olive oil plays an essential part. Vegetables can make the basis of a main dish as well as being an essential part of a main course.

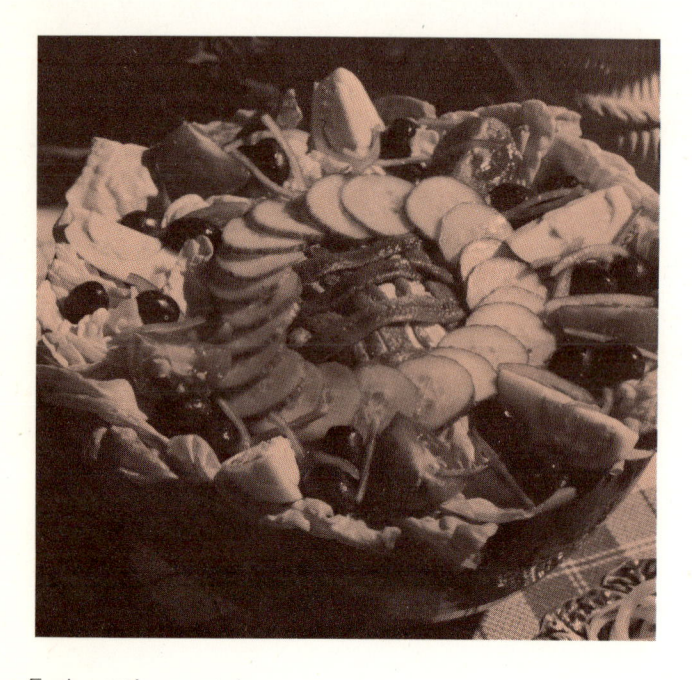

Each portion contains
170 Calories/4g carbohydrate
14g fat/9g protein
(Based on the dish serving 8)

Variation
To make a more substantial salad, add diced, cooked new potatoes and French beans.

SALAD NICOISE

for the dressing:
1 teaspoon French mustard
good pinch salt
shake black pepper
pinch garlic salt
½ — 1 teaspoon sugar
3 tablespoons Spanish olive oil
1 tablespoon white wine vinegar
1 tablespoon tarragon vinegar
1 tablespoon lemon juice
1 — 2 teaspoons chopped parsley
½ — 1 teaspoon chopped dill or fennel or pinch dried dill or fennel

1 medium can tuna fish
1 small can anchovy fillets
2 hard boiled eggs
3 — 4 tomatoes
¼ — ½ cucumber
1 small green pepper
2 — 3 sticks celery (from the heart)
1 lettuce
to garnish: black olives

Put the mustard, salt, pepper, garlic salt and sugar into a basin. Stir in the olive oil, then gradually blend in the vinegars, lemon juice and herbs. Open the cans of tuna and anchovy fillets. Pour any surplus oil from the cans into the dressing. Flake the tuna fish, chop half the anchovy fillets, mix with the tuna. Save the remaining fillets to garnish the salad. Shell the eggs and cut into quarters. Cut the tomatoes into wedges.
Slice the cucumber thinly and put into the dressing. Chop the green pepper, discard core and seeds, and the celery. Arrange the washed and dried lettuce in a salad bowl. Mix the fish with half the quartered egg, most of the tomato wedges, *half* the cucumber slices, the dressing, all the pepper and celery. Spoon on to the lettuce and top with the rest of the cucumber slices, egg, tomato, black olives and anchovy fillets.

SERVES 4 as a main dish, 6 — 8 as an hors d'oeuvre

SPANISH ONION AND OLIVE SALAD

for the dressing:
1 — 2 cloves garlic
3 tablespoons Spanish olive oil
½ teaspoon finely grated lemon rind
1½ tablespoons lemon juice
seasoning
1 teaspoon sugar

2 medium or 1 large Spanish onion
1 Cos lettuce
3 hard boiled eggs
2 — 3 tomatoes
about 12 black olives

Peel and crush the cloves garlic. Blend with the olive oil, lemon rind and juice, seasoning and sugar.
Peel the onions or onion, cut into thin slices then separate each slice into rings. Wash and dry the lettuce, break into pieces and put into a bowl. Shell and quarter the eggs and cut the tomatoes into wedges.
Mix with the lettuce. Add the onion rings and olives. Spoon the dressing over the salad just before serving and toss lightly.
This salad is delicious as an hors d'oeuvre or with cold ham.

SERVES 4

Each portion contains
260 Calories/7g carbohydrate
24g fat/5g protein

CAESAR SALAD

2 large slices bread
2 tablespoons Spanish olive oil
1 lettuce
1 clove garlic
¼ cucumber
2 — 3 tomatoes
2 hard boiled eggs
4 — 5 tablespoons mayonnaise (qv)
1 — 2 oz grated Cheddar cheese
small can anchovy fillets

Cut the crusts from the bread and cut the crumb into small dice. Heat the olive oil and fry the croûtons of bread until crisp and golden brown. Lift the croûtons out of the pan and allow to cool on absorbent paper. Wash and dry the lettuce, shred fairly finely.
Halve the garlic clove and rub round the salad bowl. Slice the cucumber, tomatoes and eggs, mix with the lettuce and put into the bowl. Top with the mayonnaise, cheese and anchovy fillets. Add the croûtons of bread just before serving the salad.

SERVES 4

Each portion contains
545 Calories/16g carbohydrate
49g fat/12g protein

RICE STUFFED PEPPERS

4 peppers (green, yellow or red)
water
seasoning
1½ tablespoons Spanish olive oil
1 — 2 onions
4 tomatoes
2 oz long grain rice
6 oz grated Cheddar cheese
to serve: tomato sauce (see recipe under Spaghetti Milanaise)
to garnish: watercress

Halve the peppers, remove cores and seeds. Put into about 1 pint boiling seasoned water with ½ tablespoon of the oil. Cook steadily for 10 — 15 minutes until tender but still fairly firm; drain well. Meanwhile heat the remaining oil in a pan. Fry the peeled chopped onions and tomatoes for 3 — 4 minutes, add the rice, mix well then add 12 tablespoons water and seasoning. Bring to the boil, stir briskly, cover the pan and simmer for 15 minutes, until the rice is tender and the liquid absorbed. Stir in most of the cheese and spoon the rice mixture into the pepper cases. Pour the hot tomato sauce into a dish, add the filled pepper cases, top with remaining cheese. Heat for a few minutes under the grill. Garnish with watercress.

SERVES 4

Each portion contains
455 Calories/9g carbohydrate
26g fat/13g protein

100

DESSERTS AND BAKING

Olive oil can be used in many desserts and kinds of cakes, etc. Suggestions for other uses of olive oil in baking are included under the recipes in this section. Weigh and measure ingredients carefully when baking so you have the correct balance of ingredients.
Check oven settings against the directions given by the manufacturer, since ovens vary a great deal.

STRAWBERRY PANCAKES

for the batter:
4 oz flour, plain or self-raising
pinch salt
1 egg
½ pint milk or milk and water
½ tablespoon Spanish olive oil
for the filling:
2 tablespoons redcurrant jelly
2 tablespoons water
squeeze lemon juice (optional)
8 oz small strawberries
to fry the pancakes: 2 – 3 tablespoons Spanish olive oil

Sieve the flour and salt into a bowl. Add the egg and milk or milk and water gradually and beat into a smooth batter. Whisk in the oil just before cooking (this helps to produce deliciously crisp pancakes). Meanwhile prepare the filling. Put the jelly, water and lemon juice into a saucepan, stir over a low heat until the jelly has dissolved. Add the fruit and keep hot; do not allow to boil. Pour enough oil into a frying pan or crêpe (pancake) pan to give a thin coating. Heat this, then spoon or pour in enough batter to give a paper thin coating. Cook for approximately 2 minutes over a fairly high heat, toss or turn and cook on the second side. Tip on to a *hot* plate and fill with a little strawberry mixture. Keep the pancakes hot in a low oven, or over a pan of boiling water. Continue like this until all the pancakes are made.

Makes about 8 pancakes

Each pancake contains
205 Calories/19g carbohydrate
13g fat/3g protein

101

APPLE FRITTERS

for the batter:
4 oz self-raising flour (or plain flour with 1 teaspoon baking powder)
pinch salt
1 egg
¼ pint milk
3 tablespoons water
½ tablespoon Spanish olive oil

2 — 3 large cooking apples
little flour
for frying: Spanish olive oil (see method)
to coat: caster sugar (optional)

Sieve the flour or flour and baking powder with the salt. Beat in the egg, milk, water and oil. (Omit water if you like a thicker coating; the olive oil helps to give crisp coating.) Whisk the batter again just before using. Peel and core the apples and cut into slices about ¼ — ½ inch in thickness; pat on absorbent paper to dry the fruit. Coat in flour (this helps the batter to adhere to the apple slices). Fry in hot shallow or deep oil (see fried fish section for details of testing oil temperature) for 6 — 8 minutes until the batter is crisp and golden and the apple slices tender. Drain on absorbent paper and dust with sugar or serve with peach sauce, as in the picture.

SERVES 4 (or serves 6 if accompanied by the sauce below)
Each portion contains
275 Calories/28g carbohydrate
17g fat/3g protein
(Based on the dish serving 6)

Variation
The Dutch make a delicious fritter batter for apples by just blending the flour, pinch salt and beer. Use beer instead of the milk and water in the recipe above and add another 2 tablespoons beer instead of the egg.

PEACH SAUCE

1 medium can halved or sliced peaches
1 lemon
1 level tablespoon cornflour
3 tablespoons sieved apricot jam
1 oz sugar (optional)

Drain the peaches, dice the fruit. Blend the syrup from the can with the finely grated lemon rind and juice. Blend with the cornflour and enough water to give just over ½ pint. Pour into a saucepan, add the jam and sugar and stir over a moderate heat until thickened and clear. Add diced peaches and heat for a few minutes. Serve hot with the fritters.

SERVES 6
Each portion contains
110 Calories/29g carbohydrate
trace fat/trace protein

Some ideas when baking

Add 1 tablespoon Spanish olive oil to each 3 lb flour when baking bread as this helps to keep the bread moist. Brush the loaves with a little olive oil before the final 'proving'; this gives a crisp crust to the bread when it is baked.
Add 1 tablespoon Spanish olive oil to each 8 oz flour when making scones.
Use the short crust pastry recipe as the basis for steamed puddings, but make the dough slightly softer than for short crust pastry. Roll out the pastry and use about three-quarters of the dough to line the basin.
Fill with prepared fruit, sugar and a little water, top with a round of pastry, cover with greased foil and steam for 2½ — 3 hours.
For a savoury pudding fill with diced steak and kidney, seasoning and a little stock or water, cover with pastry and greased foil as above and steam for at least 4 hours.

Variations
Use a mixture of diced cooked fish instead of chicken. Top with grated apple (dipped in lemon juice) instead of cheese.

SAVOURY CHOUX

¼ pint water
1 tablespoon Spanish olive oil
3 oz plain or self-raising flour
2 eggs
1 egg yolk
for the filling:
3 tablespoons mayonnaise (qv)
1 tablespoon lemon juice
1 tablespoon Spanish olive oil
8 — 12 oz cooked chicken (use light and dark meat)
1 tomato
piece cucumber
little grated cheese
to garnish: tomato, cayenne pepper or paprika, watercress

Put the water and olive oil into a saucepan, bring the water to the boil. Remove the pan from the heat and beat in the flour. Return to the heat and cook very gently, stirring all the time, until you have a smooth dry ball which leaves the sides of the pan clean. Away from the heat, beat in first one egg and then the second, and lastly as much of the egg yolk as needed to produce a smooth slightly sticky texture that can be piped if wished. Pipe or spoon into about 8 rounds on a greased and floured baking tin. Bake in the centre (or just above) of a moderately hot to hot oven, 400 — 425°F (200 — 220°C), Gas Mark 5 — 6, for 15 minutes, then lower the heat to moderate to moderately hot, 375 — 400°F (190 — 200°C), Gas Mark 4 — 5, for another 15 — 20 minutes until firm and golden. Cool away from a draught, split and remove any uncooked dough and 'dry out' the buns for a short time.
Blend the mayonnaise, lemon juice, oil, diced chicken, chopped tomato and cucumber together. Put into the buns, top with the cheese and garnish with pieces of tomato, a shake of cayenne or paprika and watercress.

Makes 8
Each bun contains
280 Calories/10g carbohydrate
21g fat/14g protein

SHORT CRUST PASTRY

Olive oil makes delicious short crust pastry.
You do not have to 'rub in', as with fat, so apart from the good results it is ideal for elderly people who suffer from rheumatism, etc. and who have problems in handling ordinary pastry.

8 oz flour, preferably plain
pinch salt
4 fluid oz — 6 tablespoons Spanish olive oil
approximately 1 tablespoon cold water

Sieve the flour and salt, add the oil and gradually stir in enough water to bind. Roll out and use in any recipe.

Variations
The above recipe gives a delicious and very short pastry. For a slightly less rich pastry use 3½ fluid oz — 5¼ tablespoons Spanish olive oil and just over 1 tablespoon water to bind. To make a rich sweet pastry for flans, etc., use the richer recipe; add 1 oz caster sugar to the flour and bind with an egg yolk plus a very few drops water if required.

Richer pastry contains
1920 Calories/200g carbohydrate
122g fat/19g protein

SPONGE CAKE

1 tablespoon Spanish olive oil
1 tablespoon water
3 eggs
4 oz caster sugar
3 oz self-raising flour

Brush two 7 — 8 inch sandwich tins with a little oil and dust with flour. Put the oil and water into a basin and stand in a warm place, i.e. the warming drawer of the cooker. Whisk the eggs and sugar until thick (you should see the trail of the whisk). Sieve the flour twice, fold into the egg mixture with a metal spoon then fold in the oil and water. Pour the sponge mixture into the tins and bake for 12 — 15 minutes above the centre of a moderate oven, 375°F (190°C), Gas Mark 5, until firm to the touch. Turn out on to a wire cooling tray and cool then sandwich together with jam, etc. This cake keeps moist for up to 2 days.
It is ideal for filling with jam or fruit and cream.

Each cake contains
1160 Calories/180g Carbohydrate
44g fat/24 g protein

FRUIT PIES

Short crust pastry, made as above, rolls out easily to make fruit or savoury pies or tarts. For a 2 pint pie dish use pastry made with 6 oz flour, etc.

FRUIT CAKE

This is particularly easy to make, as there is no need to cream or beat the mixture. Measure the ingredients carefully; the mixture may seem rather soft before baking but this is quite in order.

8 oz self-raising flour (or plain flour with 2 level teaspoons baking powder)
6 oz caster sugar
8 oz mixed dried fruit
4 fluid oz — 6 tablespoons Spanish olive oil
2 tablespoons milk
2 large eggs

Mix all the ingredients together thoroughly. Brush a 7-inch round cake tin with a little olive oil; flour lightly. Put in the mixture and bake in the centre of a moderate oven, 350°F (180°C), Gas Mark 4, for a total of approximately 1¼ hours, until firm to the touch; reduce the heat slightly after 40 minutes if the cake is becoming too brown. Cool for 2 — 3 minutes in the tin then turn out on to a wire cooling tray.

Each cake contains
3260 Calories/474g carbohydrate
136g fat/36g protein

Variation
Economy Cake Use only 3 fluid oz — 4½ tablespoons olive oil, 1 egg and 4 — 6 oz dried fruit. The sugar may be reduced to 4 oz, but sugar helps to produce a light cake so do not reduce the quantity too drastically. Increase the milk to 5½ tablespoons and bake at 350 — 375°F (180 — 190°C), Gas Mark 4 — 5 for about 1 hour.

DOUGHNUTS

½ oz fresh yeast or 2 teaspoons dried yeast
3 teaspoons sugar
¼ pint warm milk plus 2½ tablespoons warm water or use all water
12 oz plain flour
pinch salt
1 tablespoon Spanish olive oil
to fill: jam
to fry: Spanish olive oil
to coat: caster sugar

Cream fresh yeast with 1 teaspoon of the sugar, add the liquid and a sprinkling of flour. If using dried yeast dissolve 1 teaspoon of the sugar in the liquid, sprinkle yeast on top, leave for 10 minutes, then mix together, add the sprinkling of flour and continue as below. Leave liquid until covered with bubbles (about 10 – 15 minutes). Sieve flour and salt, add the remaining sugar, oil and yeast liquid. Knead lightly until a smooth elastic dough. Add a little extra warm liquid if the dough seems too dry. Leave the dough in a covered bowl for about 1½ – 1¾ hours, until double its size. Knead again; divide into 12 round balls. Make an indent in each ball with a floured finger, put in a little jam then re-roll the balls. Leave on a warmed oiled baking tray for 15 – 20 minutes to begin to rise. Meanwhile heat the pan of olive oil to 365°F (185°C) with the frying basket in position. (See fried fish section for details of oil testing.) Lower some of the balls into the hot oil, fry steadily for 8 – 10 minutes, lift out of the oil, drain on absorbent paper, then roll in sugar. Fry remaining balls.

MAKES 12

Each doughnut contains
200 Calories/29g carbohydrate
9g fat/2g protein

BAKING POWDER DOUGHNUTS

8 oz self-raising flour (or plain flour and 2 teaspoons baking powder)
pinch salt
1 tablespoon Spanish olive oil
1 tablespoon sugar
1 egg
milk to mix

jam, Spanish olive oil, caster sugar — as left

Sieve the flour or flour and baking powder and salt, add the olive oil and sugar. Bind with the egg and enough milk to make an elastic dough (rather like a soft scone dough). Roll into balls, add jam and proceed as above, but do not 'prove' as yeast dough.

MAKES 8

Each doughnut contains
255 Calories/32g carbohydrate
14g fat/3g protein

Variation

Both the yeast dough and baking powder dough can be rolled out to make ring doughnuts. Roll out on a floured board to 1-inch in thickness, cut into rings. Put the yeast dough to 'prove' (as first recipe) for 15 – 20 minutes then fry, but fry the baking powder doughnuts as soon as you wish.

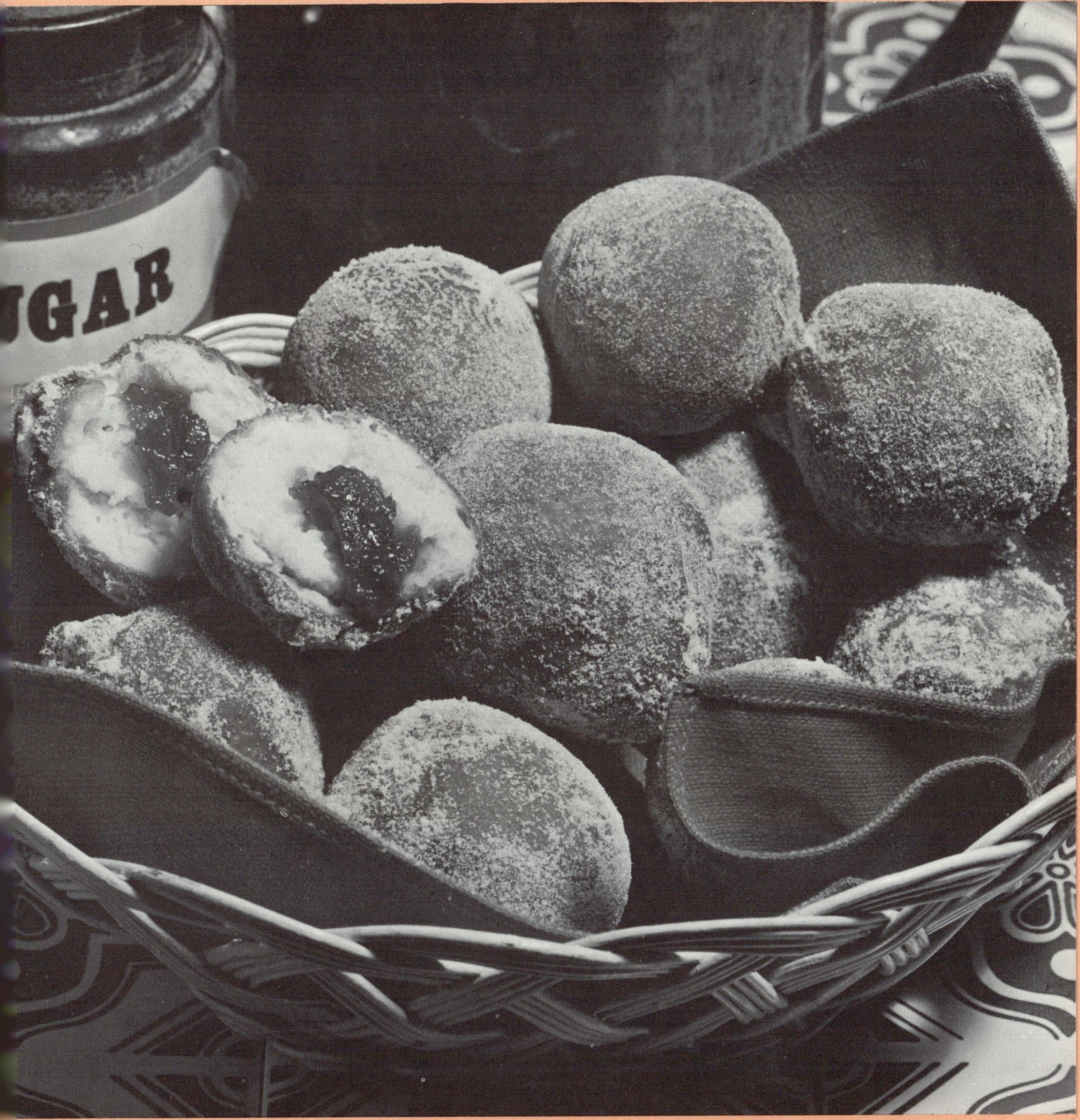

Chef G. G. Pedri of The Ivy Restaurant

TRUITE MARINEE IVY

Thoroughly clean six fresh river trout, wash and dry. Season and flour. Cover the bottom of a frying pan with olive oil. When the oil is hot, cook the trout slowly for about six minutes on each side.

Marinade
8 fl oz olive oil
1 glass dry white wine
2 glasses Dufrais vinegar
2 medium size onions
1 red pimento
thyme, origan, bay leaf
crushed peppercorn and parsley

Place the olive oil, finely sliced onions and diced pimento in a saucepan and cook until the onions are light golden in colour. Add the wine, vinegar, pepper and herbs and boil for 15 minutes. Remove from stove and add a pinch of finely chopped parsley. Pour over the trout and leave for 24 hours. Serve cold.

SERVES 6

THE IVY has been a favourite restaurant of the theatrical profession for over half a century. Its founder, Abel Giandellini, started a small restaurant in the West End at the turn of the century with the intention of making it the rendezvous for those of discriminating taste, the famous not only in the theatre but arts and politics, too.
He succeeded. Prime Ministers from Lloyd George to Winston Churchill have dined regularly at The Ivy.
The great Cochran revue star, Alice Delysia, unwittingly named the restaurant when she assured Abel that she and the restaurant would 'cling together like the ivy'.
Its loyal supporters through the 20s and 30s included such celebrities as Edgar Wallace, Noel Coward, Marie Tempest, George Robey, Gracie Fields, Ivor Novello, Epstein, Sybil Thorndike and Rex Harrison. By the Second World War The Ivy's reputation had spread across the Atlantic and into Europe. In fact, after nearly 70 years The Ivy is now something of an institution with the theatre very much at its heart.

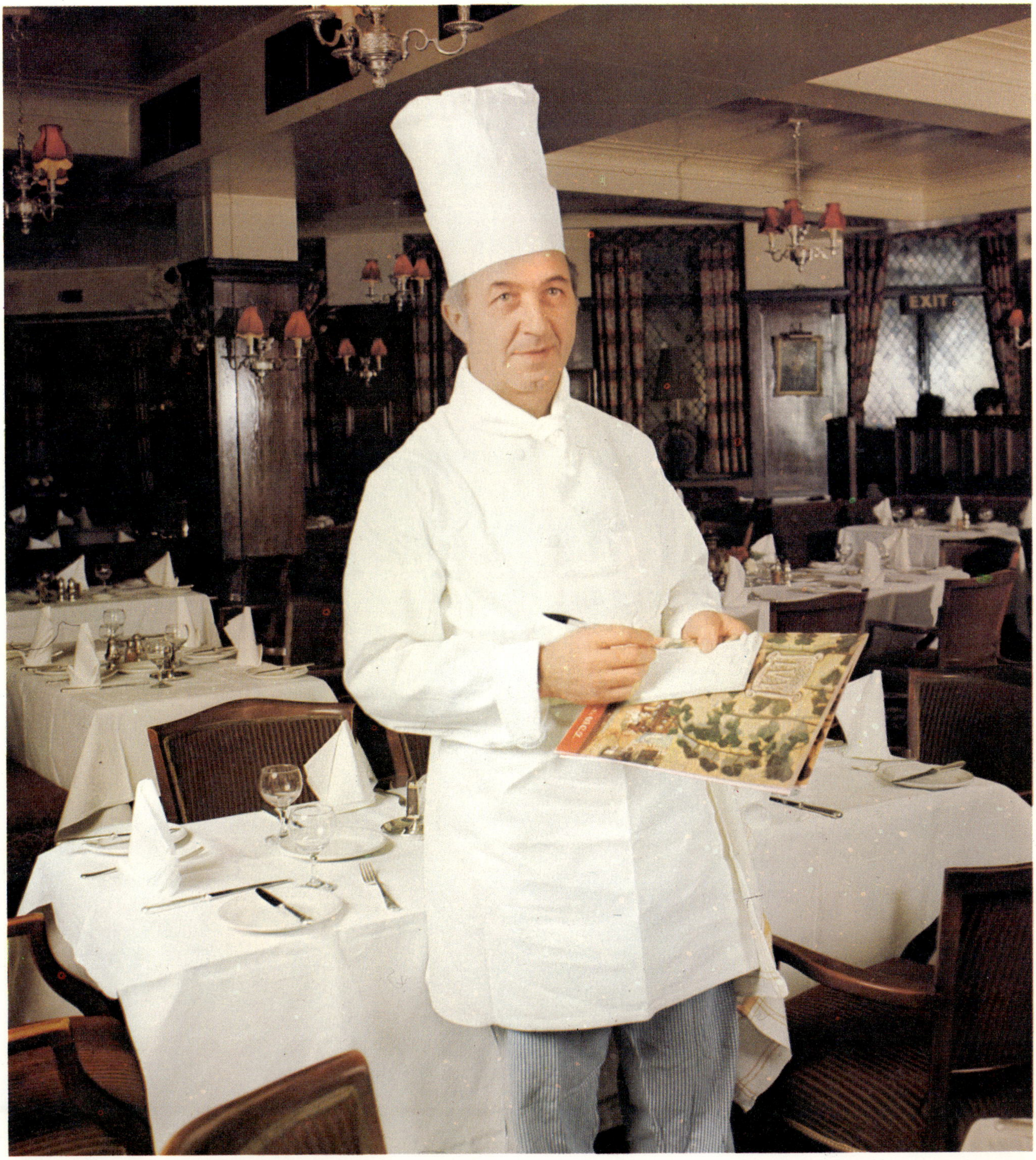
EXIT

Chef Guilio Imperato of La Napoule

SCAMPI ON SKEWER IMPERATO STYLE

1¾ lb washed and shelled scampi
24 thin slices streaky bacon
8 large ripe peeled tomatoes cut into 8 segments
3 lemons
Spanish olive oil
salt, pepper, flour, breadcrumbs
sprigs of fresh parsley

Season the scampi with salt and pepper then roll half a slice of bacon around each. Fix on a metal skewer with segment of tomato between each scampi. Dip completed skewer in flour, then olive oil and finally in breadcrumbs. Place the skewers on a dish and grill gently for about ten minutes until the scampi are golden and crisp. Serve with half a lemon and sprig of parsley for each person.

the sauce:
1 gill Spanish olive oil
1 large onion (finely chopped)
1 clove garlic (finely chopped)
12 peeled, pipped and coarsely chopped tomatoes
1 tablespoon French mustard
½ gill wine vinegar
salt and pepper

Heat the olive oil in a saucepan. Add the onion and garlic and when golden the French mustard, tomatoes, salt and pepper and finally wine vinegar.
Boil for ten minutes and serve separately in a sauce boat.
SERVES 6

For various reasons, the number of new, high-class French restaurants that have opened and survived in London's West End in the past decade are very, very few. La Napoule opened only five years ago and in that short time has won an enviable reputation, thanks to the perfect collaboration between manager Lino Armani and Chef Guilio Imperato. Leading food writers have included La Napoule in the London restaurant Top Ten list.

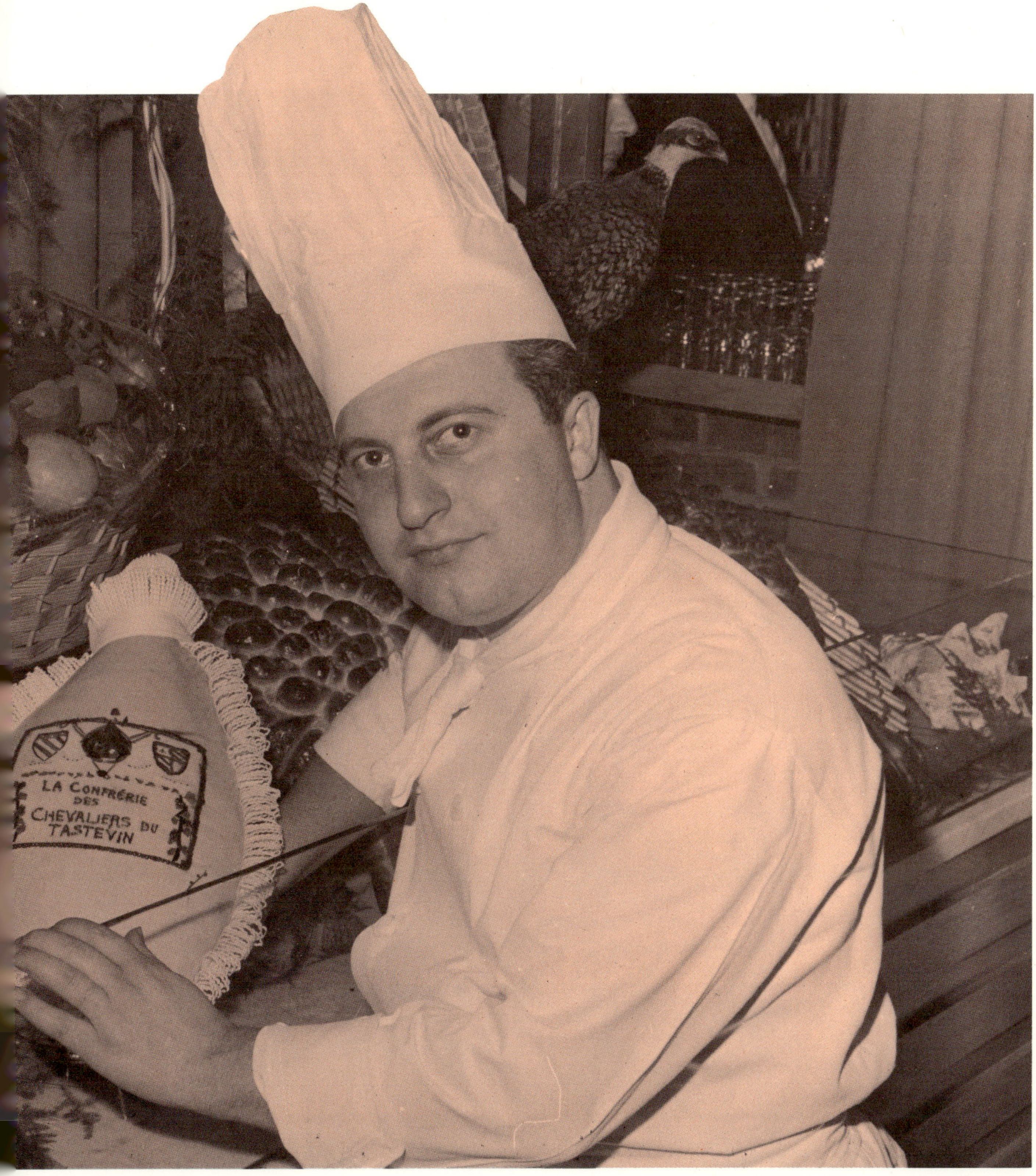
LA CONFRÉRIE
DES
CHEVALIERS DU
TASTEVIN

112

When the Caprice was opened two years after the end of the Second World War, it brought to an austerity-fed London a touch of glamour and promise of good food that had been missing for so long. It achieved popularity not by gimmicks but simply by offering fresh, well-cooked, properly served food in pleasant surroundings.
Only one thing has changed — the decor. The silk ruched walls and light fans have gone but pink is still the dominant colour, though it's softer now, more in keeping with the mood of the 70s.
It remains the restaurant that's so much a part of the contemporary London scene, the place to see and be seen in.

Chef Harry Errington of the Caprice

CURRY CAPRICE

1 onion, chopped
olive oil
1 teaspoon tomato purée
1 dessertspoon flour
1 dessertspoon sugar
1 lb chicken or meat

mince the following:
1 tablespoon chutney
1 small cooking apple, peeled and cored
1 banana
1 clove of garlic
2 oz sultanas

Fry the finely chopped onion in a little olive oil, add all the minced ingredients and cook lightly for a few minutes, stirring from time to time. Add the tomato purée, curry powder and mix well, then stir in the flour carefully.
Add the stock and sugar and simmer gently for 20 minutes. Finally add the chicken or meat to the sauce and cook for about 35 minutes. You may need to add a little stock if the sauce gets too thick. Serve with rice.

SERVES 4

Chef René Montagnon of Kettner's

TOMATOES PROVENÇALE

8 large tomatoes
3 tablespoons olive oil
1 clove garlic
1 onion,(finely chopped)
6 oz brown rice
¾ pint stock
1 tablespoon currants
8 oz minced cooked beef
salt and pepper

Cut the tops off the tomatoes and scoop out the insides. Fry the onion and garlic in olive oil until soft then add the rice. Cover the pan and simmer for about 5 minutes. Stir in the tomato pulp, currants and stock; season with salt and pepper. Cover and simmer until the rice is cooked and liquid absorbed. Stir in the meat and insert the mixture into the tomato cases. Place stuffed tomatoes in a fireproof dish and leave in a moderate oven for 20/30 minutes.

SERVES 4

Kettner's, like the one year older Café Royal, has a long and distinguished history. For more than a century, celebrities from the worlds of politics, business, the arts and sometimes royalty have patronised the restaurant. It could hardly have had a more auspicious beginning for its founder was no less than Auguste Kettner, head chef to Napoleon III. Six years after its opening in 1867, a dinner party was held there in honour of the Emperor Napoleon with Disraeli, Bulwer Lytton, Le Duc Mornay, Le Comte d'Orsay and Lord Derby as guests. Kettner's is still where it began: on the same Romilly Street, Soho, site.
Its elegant rooms are haunted by history and one of them is named the Edward Room. It is no idle choice: Edward VII really did dine there frequently.

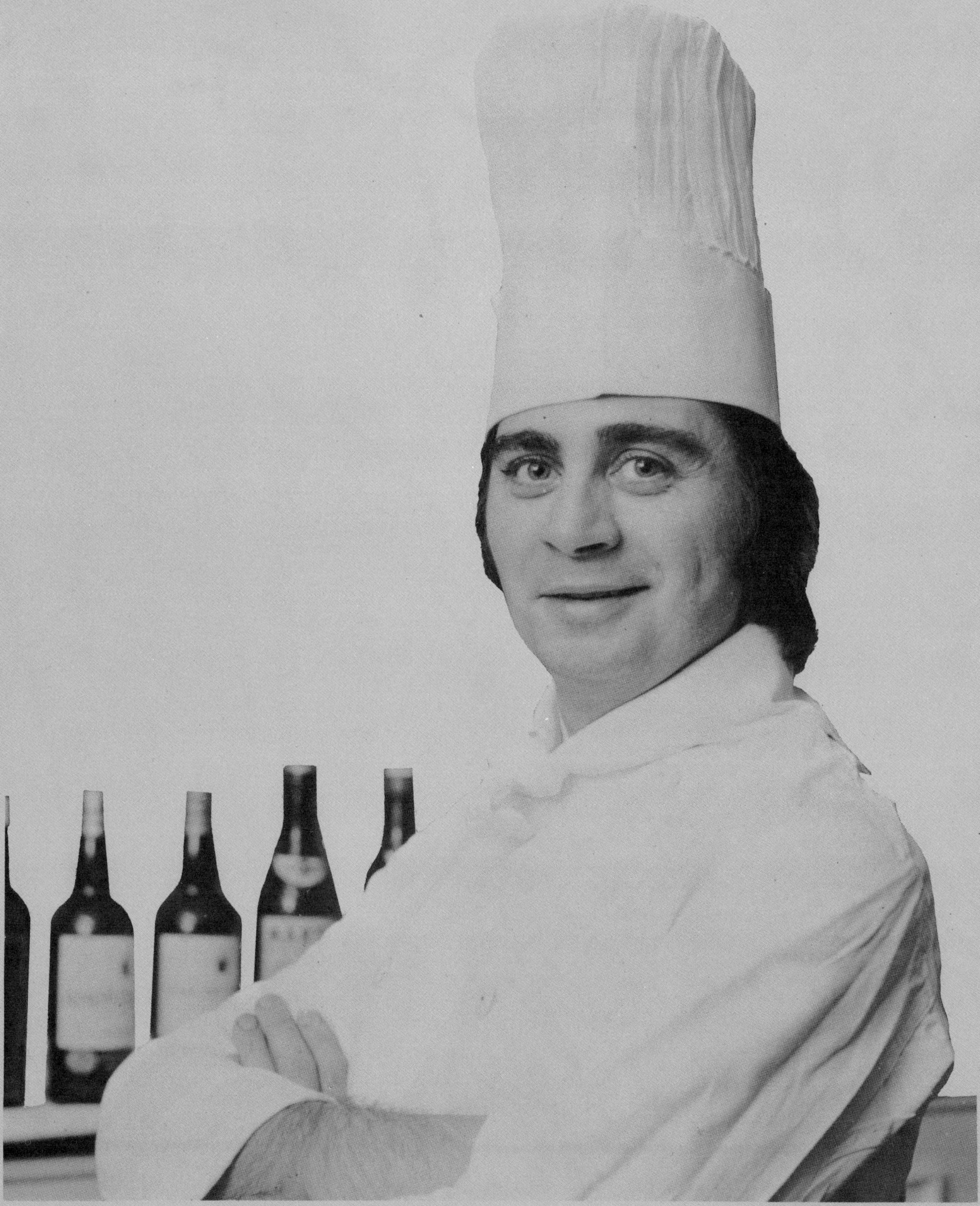

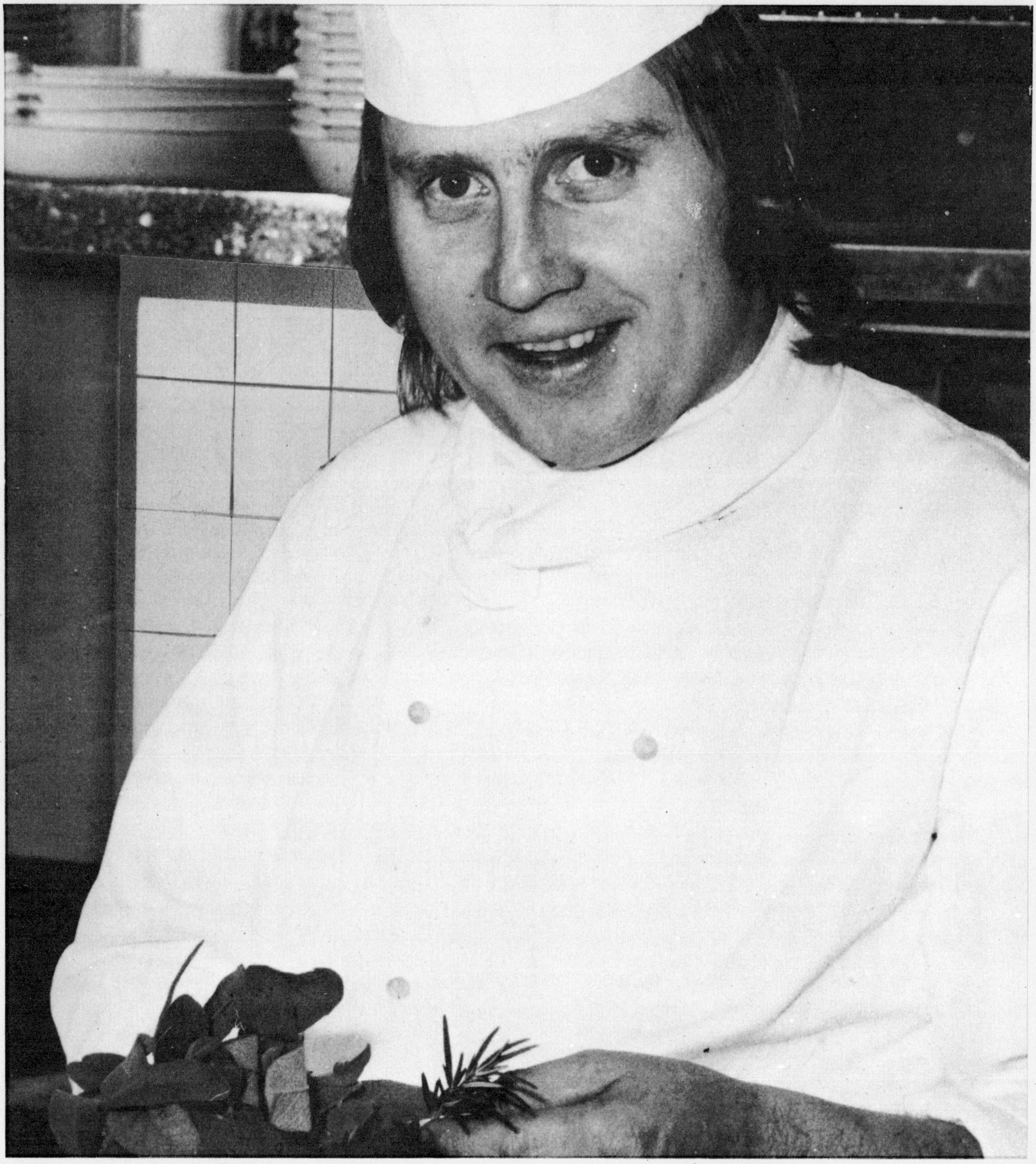

Stylish and sumptuous Walton's of Walton Street, SW3, is one of London's newest restaurants. It has been described by Egon Ronay as 'London's most sophisticated small restaurant' and also as one of its most expensive.
The menu is essentially French but it includes several 18th century English dishes.
The decor is elegant in greys and yellows. The walls in the terrace room are hung with specially designed silks and there is a tasteful combination of polished steel and antique furniture. The three separate facets are 'linked' by Italian marble tiles and the mirror room is romantically reflected in smoked glass.

Chef Ernst Stark of Waltons

HONEYED PRAWNS AND GRAPEFRUIT

for the dressing:
2 parts olive oil
1 part lemon juice
1 teaspoon honey
1 teaspoon dark rum
1 teaspoon orange juice
grated rind of one orange

for seasoning:
salt and freshly milled pepper

for the filling:
4 grapefruit
¼ lb king prawns
2 oz pecan nuts

Cut two grapefruit in half, scooping out the flesh with a dessert spoon. Remove rind and pith of other two grapefruit with a sharp knife and segment flesh. Prepare the dressing, toss in the fruit and prawns and allow to marinate for ½ hour while chilling. Dress into the grapefruit shells with a garnish of pecan nuts and spoonful of dressing.
This dressing is delicious used with any meat or fish to make an interesting salad.

Housewife's Choice

KIPPER SALAD

For the marinade:
1/3 pint Spanish olive oil
1/6 pint vinegar

4 kipper fillets
1 lettuce
½ cucumber
1 green pepper
green olives (to taste)

For the vinaigrette dressing:
1/3 pint Spanish olive oil
1/6 pint vinegar
1 teaspoon dry mustard
salt and pepper

Place kipper fillets in a shallow dish and cover with the marinade mixture. Leave overnight. When ready to serve lift out the fillets carefully and drain well. Cut into strips. Prepare the salad by washing, drying and shredding the lettuce into a bowl. De-seed and slice pepper. Add pepper, sliced cucumber and green olives. Place fillets on salad. Mix the mustard with little vinegar and season with salt and pepper. Make the vinaigrette dressing by adding remaining oil and vinegar. Mix well together and pour over salad.

SERVES 4

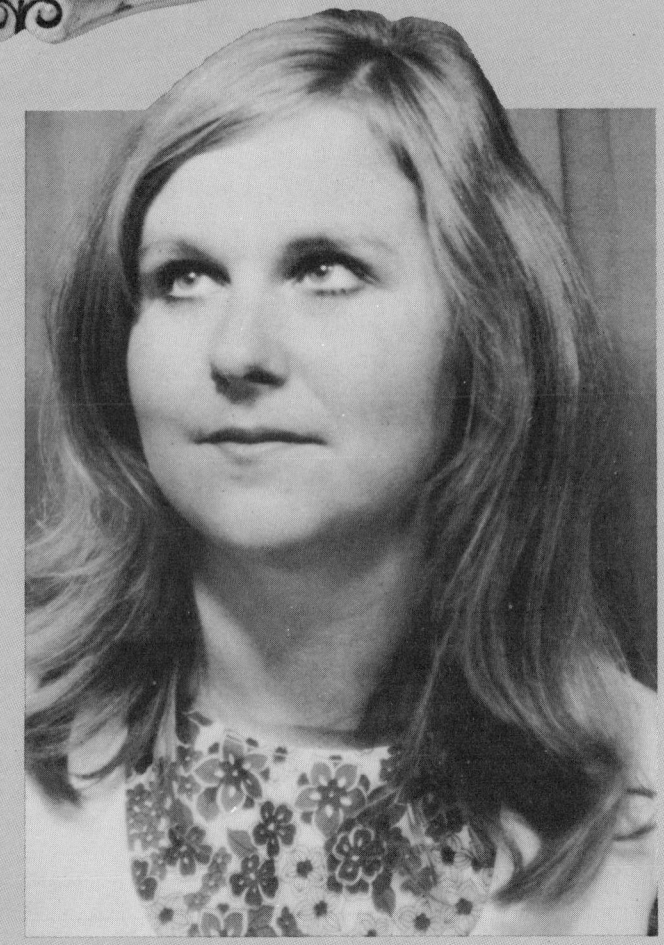

Mrs Zoe Bowman, Torquay, Devon

QUICK RISOTTO

1 large onion
1 large green pepper
tin tomatoes/tomato purée
2 — 3 oz long grain rice
½ lb cooked meat (chicken, ham, beef as preferred)
parsley

Fry onion and pepper in olive oil until cooked. Add tomatoes or tomato purée and ¾ pint of water. When it comes to the boil add the rice and mix in thoroughly. Cook until fairly dry, add chopped meat (or grated cheese). Garnish with sprigs of parsley.

Miss S R Devereux, New Barnet, Herts

Mrs F M Roos, Ham, Surrey

COD WITH ORANGE SALAD

4 cod steaks
1 oz butter
1 oz white breadcrumbs
1 oz grated cheese
3 oranges
1 tablespoon Spanish olive oil
1 teaspoon lemon juice
salt and pepper
watercress for garnish

Season fish, dot with half the butter and grill for 5 minutes. Mix breadcrumbs and cheese together. Turn fish and cover with cheese mixture. Dot with remaining butter and grill for another 5 minutes. Peel oranges, cut into thin slices and mix with olive oil and lemon juice. Arrange cod steaks on a dish, surround with oranges and garnish with watercress.

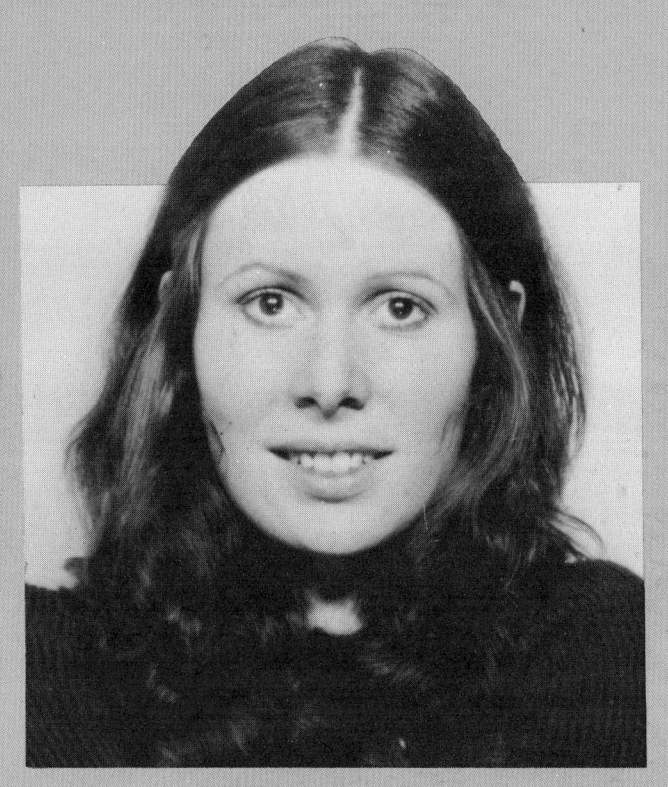

GOLDEN RICE

1 cup of long grain rice
2 cups of cold water
salt
1 teaspoon of Spanish olive oil

Put rice in saucepan with water, salt and olive oil. Bring to the boil quickly then put lid tightly on saucepan and simmer *very* gently for 20 minutes. Rice is then ready to serve.

Mrs M Gabriel, Chiswick, London

Mrs J Cunningham, Hove, Sussex

CHICKEN PEPITORIA

1 small chicken cut into portions
2 tablespoons plain flour
3 tablespoons Spanish olive oil
¼ cup blanched almonds
1 small onion (chopped)
4 tomatoes (peeled and sliced)
1 clove garlic (crushed)
good pinch saffron and curry powder
sherry

Shape the chicken joints and dust with flour. Meantime lightly brown the almonds in the olive oil then remove and set aside as garnish. Add the floured chicken to the oil and cook over fairly high heat until well browned. Reduce heat and add onion and garlic to the pan. Dissolve the saffron in sherry and add to chicken. Cover and simmer until chicken is tender (about 40 minutes). Remove chicken, pour off excess oil and place on heated dish. Garnish with tomatoes sprinkled with curry powder and almonds.

SERVES 4

MERO AL JEREZ

3 lbs halibut steak
2 tablespoons Spanish olive oil
½ cup medium sherry
1½ teaspoons salt and sprinkle of pepper
¼ cup slivered almonds
3 sprigs parsley (chopped)

Brush shallow baking dish with a little of the olive oil, place halibut in the dish and sprinkle with salt and pepper. Brush with remaining olive oil. Place almonds over top. Baste with sherry as it bakes in oven 350°F (180°C) Gas Mark 4 or until fish flakes easily. Sprinkle with parsley in last 5 minutes. Garnish with sprigs of parsley and twists of lemon.
If liked, a hint of garlic improves this dish.

SERVES 6

Mrs I C Nash, West Wickham, Kent

GINGERBREAD

8 oz plain flour
2 teaspoons ground ginger
3 oz sugar
1 teaspoon bicarbonate of soda
½ teaspoon golden raising powder
½ teaspoon baking powder
¼ teaspoon salt
2 tablespoons Spanish olive oil
2 tablespoons golden syrup
¼ pint of milk

Mix all dry ingredients thoroughly together in mixing bowl. Slightly warm syrup, olive oil and milk then add to the dry ingredients in mixing bowl. Mix thoroughly then pour immediately into a greased baking tin (10 x 7) and bake in pre-heated oven for 40 minutes at 300°F (150°C), Gas Mark 3, until golden brown. Chopped ginger can be added to mixture if desired.

Mrs P F M Hunt, Romford, Essex

Colourful can and golden bottle:
a few of the Spanish olive oil brands available in the UK

123

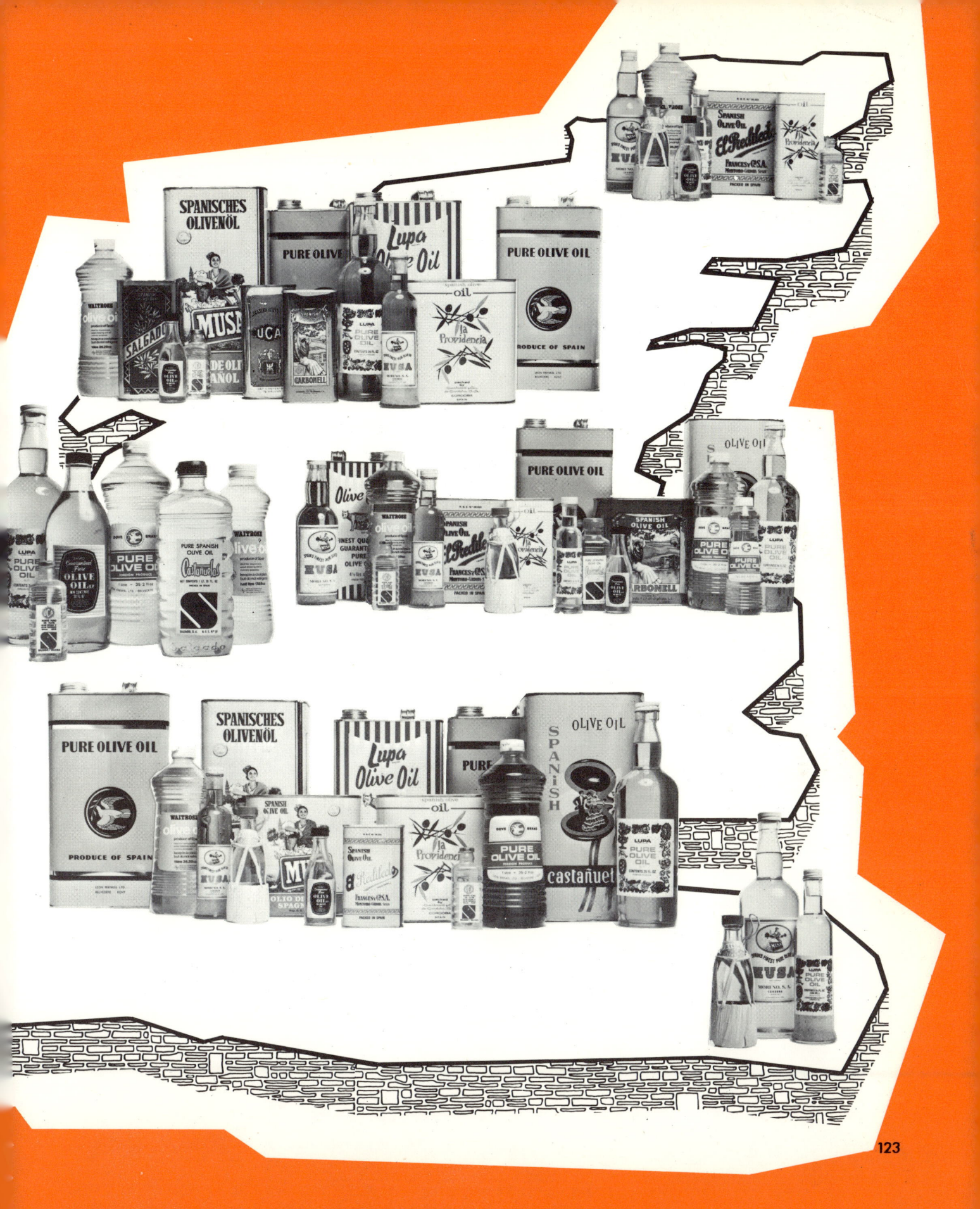

Index to Recipes

Starters

Artichokes with Lemon Mayonnaise 71
Avocado Dip 32
Avocado Vinaigrette 71
Bortsch 32
Caldo Verde a Terheiro 30
Cheese and Carrot Soup 70
Courgettes Provencal 30
Gazpacho 37
Mayonnaise 75
(Fennel/Green/Lemon/Tomato
and Tartare Sauce)
Mushrooms Malaga 35
Pierozki 35
Pizza alla Napoletana 72
Salsa Guasacaca 34
Seafood Cocktail Caprice 74
Stuffed Mushrooms 73
Taramasalata 37
Tomatoes a la Greque 38
Vichyssoise 70

Fish

Bouillabaisse a la Parisienne (and Rouille) 40/1
Curried Fish Scallops 77
Perfect Fried Fish 76
Perfect Fried Potatoes 77
Poached Skate with Herbed Rice 78
Russian Fish Pasty 41
Stuffed Codling 78
Truite Nicoise 42
Valencia Pancakes 43

Meat

Barbecued Steak 81
Beef with Oranges 83
Beef Rissoles 86
Beef Stroganoff 44
Caribbean Kebabs 44
Chilli con Carne 45
Curried Veal Risotto 86
Enchillados 48
Goulash 47
Moussaka 47
Pepperpot Pork 49
Pork and Cranberry Kebabs 84
Pork Chop Suey 49
Pork and Red Cabbage Casserole 50
Savoury Meat Ring 89
Scaloppine alla Bolognese 80
Scotch Cutlets with Mint Jelly 85
Spicy Steak 82
Stuffed Pork Polonaise 50
Sukiyaki 52
Sweet and Sour Pork 52
Sweet and Sour Meat Balls 88
Veal Goulash 82
Veal St Lucia 54

Poultry and game

Cherry Blossom Chicken 56
Chicken Lahore 56
Chicken Mandarin 58
Chicken Maryland 59
Fried Chicken and Herbs 90
Jugged Hare 92
Lemon Chicken 91

Pasta, rice and egg dishes

Biber Dolmas and Yalanci Dolmas 60
Garlic Eggs 60
Paella 97
Peppered Eggs 94
Risotto 61
Savoury Eggs 95
Spaghetti Bolognese 93

Spaghetti Milanaise 96
Spaghetti Milanaise with Meat Balls 96
Spanish Omelette 95
Spanish Rice 63
Tomato Omelette 63

Salads and vegetables

Caesar Salad 99
Insalata Olives 64
Mexican Salad 65
Portuguese Salad 65
Rice Stuffed Peppers 100
Salad Nicoise 98
Spanish Onion and Olive Salad 99

Desserts and baking

Apple Fritters 102
Doughnuts and Baking Powder Doughnuts 106
Fruit Cake and Economy Cake 105
Fruit Pies 104
Peach Sauce 102
Savoury Choux 103
Short Crust Pastry 104
Sponge Cake 104
Strawberry Pancakes 101

**Index to recipes in
Around the world in 40 dishes
Home cooking with olive oil**

Conversion table

1 oz = 28.4 grammes(g)
1 pint = .57 litre(l)
1 lb = 454.4 grammes(g)

Photo credits

British Meat Service (Meat and Livestock Commission)
British Egg Information Service
US Rice Council
Tabasco Pepper Sauce
Angel Studios

Among those present . . .

G C B Andrew
Writer, former journalist, industrial editor and publicist, Gilmore Andrew has contributed articles and news stories to scores of newspapers and journals since the late 40s. He has written all manner of things from clerihews for the New York Herald Tribune to sports reports for the BBC and national press, from industrial film scripts to advertisement copy. He spent ten years in industry as a publicist and a similar time as a director of a London advertising agency. He is a Fellow and former National Chairman of the British Association of Industrial Editors, Member of the Institute of Practitioners in Advertising (1967/73), Member of the Institute of Public Relations and British Industrial Marketing Association.

Raymond E Meylan
After a spell as creative director of major advertising agencies, Ray Meylan set up his own design unit, Artes Graphicae, in the late 50s. His regular clients now include many national and international concerns, among them ICI, Courtaulds, Du Pont, GPO, Cubitts, BP, Metal Box, NEDO and NSPCC. His unit's design range is extensive: magazines, advertisements, posters, books, exhibition stands and displays, company symbols and a variety of print.
He has designed and produced many books and annuals on various subjects. In the culinary category are the Robert Carrier Mini Cookbook series, British Weight-Watchers Cookery Book No. 1, Personal Choice and the latest to appear, The Children's Cookery Book. In 1970, in face of strong international competition, he won the contract to design and produce the official book commemorating the 2000th anniversary of the Persian Empire. The Shah personally sent copies to 200 heads of state.